CALIFORNIA
SPLENDOR

KATHRYN MASSON

Photography by DAVID GLOMB

Foreword by BOB GALE

RIZZOLI
NEW YORK

New York · Paris · London · Milan

To JOHN and GLORIA CARSWELL—

true friends, delightful companions,
and interesting architecture connoisseurs,
whose generosity and kindness
over the past forty years have added great joy to my life.

First published in the United States of America in 2013 by
RIZZOLI INTERNATIONAL PUBLICATIONS, INC.
300 Park Avenue South, New York, NY 10010
www.rizzoliusa.com

ISBN-13: 978-0-8478-3965-0

Library of Congress Control Number: 2013933284

Distributed to the U.S. Trade by Random House, New York

Designed by Abigail Sturges Graphic Design

Printed and bound in China

2013 2014 2015 2016 2017 2018 / 10 9 8 7 6 5 4 3 2 1

PAGE 1   *Crocker-Fagan Mansion, Pebble Beach,
George Washington Smith, architect, Byzantine style, 1928*

PAGES 2 AND 3   El Fureidis, *Montecito, Bertram G. Goodhue,
architect, Classical Revival style, 1906*

CONTENTS

CALIFORNIA SPLENDOR:
A PERSONAL JOURNEY

*I*f you're a religious fundamentalist, *put this book down immediately!* Otherwise, you'll risk breaking the Tenth Commandment, "Thou shalt not covet thy neighbor's house." For everyone else, welcome to California.

California. It's our one state that can be called mythic. As Humphrey Bogart said about the Maltese Falcon, it's "the stuff that dreams are made of." And when you combine the things that California embodies—its spectacular geography, its comfortable climate, its visionary characters with outsized personalities, its "bigger is better" mentality, its endless possibilities, and the fortunes that have been made—you get a lot of jaw-dropping, awe-inspiring homes. You get *California Splendor.*

My first experience with California Splendor was summer, 1962. I was eleven years old, on a family vacation—a road trip, from St. Louis. We visited Hearst Castle. I knew nothing about the man or the property. But we took the tour, and I saw that swimming pool. And that's when I broke the Tenth Commandment. *I wanted to swim in that pool.*

"Any questions?" asked the guide.

My little hand shot up like a rocket. "Does anybody ever get to swim in this pool?"

"Yes. Twice a year, the tour guides have a party, and we all get to swim in it."

Whoa. Here was an employment opportunity that I had never considered.

Soon an even more compelling argument for this vocation presented itself when we viewed the indoor Neptune Pool. *As a tour guide, I'd get to swim in this pool, too!*

Although my flirtation with this career path was short-lived, the story has a happy ending because, 48 years later, as result of involvement with the Hearst Castle Preservation Foundation, I finally did get to swim in both of those pools. (And yes, it was amazing!)

My next memorable encounter with California Splendor involves two homes in this volume. In fall 1984, we were scouting locations for *Back to the Future*, specifically Doc Brown's mansion. I don't recall who suggested the Gamble House in Pasadena, but it took less than two seconds to see that it was perfect. (For the record, the Tenth Commandment does not prohibit coveting historic buildings that are maintained for the benefit of the public.) The icing on the cake was that it had never been used as a location in a Hollywood film before: we'd be the first. But we had to convince the managers of that historic property that we would do no harm. They were understandably skeptical. After all, we were those awful Hollywood people about whom everyone has a hor-

ror story. They had to review our script to ensure there was no sex, no violence, and nothing off-color. The shooting conditions would be restrictive. We were limited as to where and when we could film. And one thing was absolutely forbidden: filming inside the house. That meant we had to find another location with an interior that matched the look of the Gamble House. Luckily, architects Greene and Greene had built another breathtaking mansion nearby: The Blacker House.

Back then, the Blacker House was owned by Marjorie Hill, widow of Max Hill. Now nearly broke, she was overjoyed to have us film inside because she needed the money. This too was a filmic first—no one had ever shot inside (or outside) this mansion either. A few months later, we had to return to reshoot our scenes, only to learn that Marjorie had been forced to sell the house. Luckily, escrow hadn't closed, and we scrambled to get in there before the deadline, making it with just two days to spare.*

Fast-forward to 1989. We were in preproduction on our sequels. For *Back to the Future Part III*, we wanted to run our opening titles over another exterior shot of the Gamble House. This

---

* The new owners gutted the house and sold off all of the Greene and Greene fixtures in an event known in Pasadena as the rape of the Blacker House. This crime against architecture resulted in a city ordinance to prevent a similar occurrence. Thankfully, the current owners went to great lengths to successfully restore the home to its original glory.

David B. Gamble House, Pasadena, Charles and Henry Greene, Greene and Greene, architects, Craftsman style, 1907–1909

Robert R. Blacker House, San Marino, Henry Greene and Charles Greene, architects, Arts and Crafts style, 1907

time, we were welcomed with open arms. Everyone there had loved *Back to the Future*, and they'd been especially impressed with how beautiful we'd made the house look. Furthermore, the film had generated more visitors and tremendous positive interest in the property. *Of course* we could shoot another exterior! Not only that, we were invited to shoot inside. We would be the *only* movie ever to film in their rooms. We eagerly scouted the interior, lusting over the images we could create and thinking of what a major coup this would be. But a few minutes later, director Robert Zemeckis and I looked at each other with the same realization: a film company, even one as responsible as ours, would do serious damage to this irreplaceable gem. And that was something we just couldn't live with. So we turned down that historic opportunity, built our own Greene and Greene–inspired sets, and never lost a minute of sleep over it.

The success of those films provided my wife Tina and me with the ability to attain our own bit of California Splendor, called *Mira Vista*, which you can experience vicariously starting on page 36. How's that for the greatest ending ever?

Julius Shulman, the dean of architectural photography, observed that more people experience architecture through photography than through the architecture itself. He was right. So, with the splendorous vision and illuminating text of author Kathryn Masson accompanied by the outstanding imagery of photographer David Glomb, prepare to experience the majesty of *California Splendor*. Oh, and if you happen to break the Tenth Commandment…? Join the club!

BOB GALE
Co-creator of the acclaimed Back to the Future *film trilogy*

LEFT *David B. Gamble House, Pasadena, Charles and Henry Greene, architects, Craftsman style, 1907–1909*

OPPOSITE Wildwood, *Piedmont, Bernard Maybeck, architect, 1911*

PREFACE

*W*hat a privilege and thrill it has been to spend time in these magnificent houses. They are my personal choices and are, of course, only a selection of some of California's greatest houses. Others were not included because they had not been restored and were in ruins, showed evidence of unfortunate remodelings, or remained off-limits by their private owners. I am grateful to those owners who gave up some of their privacy to share their homes. The 17 houses in this book exemplify a range of styles, building materials, architects, and sites that illustrate the diversity of California architecture built for those with means from the mid-nineteenth century to the mid-twentieth century.

The joy of making a book like this is in the moments. I thoroughly enjoyed working with photographer David Glomb. Three days at Hearst Castle, climbing, climbing, here and there, discovering places off the beaten path (with an official escort, of course). An entire day soaking in the beauty of the Blacker House, feeling the mood of the interior change with the sunlit reflections through the art-glass windows. Revisiting the elegant rooms in the Leland Stanford Mansion and imagining the early days of Sacramento. Sitting on the patio with John Saladino, relishing the conversation and balmy Santa Barbara weather. Watching David Glomb's jaw drop as he walked in stockinged feet into the magnificent great room at Wildwood. He looked at me. "I know, I know," is all I could say. Touching base with Rizzoli editor Douglas Curran after a day's incredible work. "Wait till you see

these images. You are going to die!" Standing in the cloister of a Byzantine mansion in Pebble Beach—a dream.

A number of the houses in the book are private residences whose owners could not have been prouder of their restoration and renovation work that often ran into the millions of dollars. These visionary individuals have done more than create beautiful homes for themselves. They have given us all the gift of preserving great works of architecture that may be enjoyed for future generations.

The houses that are now museums are gifts to the public, made possible by the foresight of the original owners and/or foundations and the amazing staffs who care for and raise funds for the continued conservation of these California treasures. How these organizations have grown attests to the importance of the museums. Hopefully, the current economic condition in California will improve and all of the historic properties owned by the state and administered by its parks system will again be open full-time. The staff of the Leland Stanford Mansion State Historic Park has been entrusted with one of California's architectural glories. With its multi-million-dollar restoration, any visitor will surely feel the opulence of the Gold Rush era. It is not to be missed. And regarding the Hearst Castle, another property owned by the State of California, what can I say? If you haven't already seen it, go!

My hope in producing and writing this book is that the museum houses will be visited and the private residences experienced through the pictures and accompanying text.

Here's to California, land of promise.

LEFT *Carson Mansion, Eureka, Samuel and Joseph Cather Newsom, architects, Queen Anne style, 1884–1886.* Photo by Paul Rocheleau, courtesy of Paul Rocheleau Studios.

OPPOSITE Mi Sueño, *Coppell Mansion, Beverly Hills, Bertram G. Goodhue, architect, Spanish Baroque and Spanish Colonial Revival styles, 1915.* Photo by Romy Wyllie.

INTRODUCTION

California is truly the land of opportunity. The rich soil and mild climate, along with the discovery of gold and the social culture that evolved in cities and towns, brought new residents from all over the world. Some were captains of industry who came to the state to retire and enjoy the land of plenty. Others who ventured west were industrious men who initially came to California for various reasons and turned their ideas and investments into great monetary successes. They and their heirs built magnificent houses on grand spreads of land to announce their elevated status in society and to satisfy their desire to own the finest, most luxurious homes of their day. They hired preeminent architects and constructed their mansions on the most prominent parcels. They embraced the leading architectural styles of their day, including Victorian Italianate, period revival, Arts and Crafts, Beaux-Arts, Neoclassical, Spanish Colonial Revival, and European vernacular, often producing "ultimate" versions of the genre. Today's conscientious, preservation-minded owners have restored and conserved these iconic houses and honored the structures by listing them on the National Register of Historic Places. Many of the houses are protected by their designations as state or national landmarks. Through their architecture, these houses educate us by representing a distinct time and place in California's history.

Beginning in the early 1830s, fertile land beckoned farmers from the Midwest and East Coast with the possibility of a new life, despite the months of slow overland travel it took

to reach California. After the Mexican government began to secularize the mission system in 1833, those vast holdings became available for private ownership. Wealthy Mexican families and a handful of Anglo-Americans were granted tracts of land or *ranchos*, the acreage of which was measured in the thousands and used mainly for grazing cattle.

Everything, including agriculture, changed dramatically after the influx of thousands of gold seekers from all over the world from early 1849 through 1860. In 1849 alone, the population of California grew from 26,000 to 92,000. It then grew steadily until, by 1860, it had reached 300,000. Farming methods changed, irrigation systems were developed, and new technologies met the increasing demand for food. In 1872, nonirrigated wheat was the chief crop, but by the 1890s agriculture was geared toward fruits, nuts, and vegetables, products that required intensive irrigation systems. The transportation improvements that fueled the phenomenal growth of cities and towns throughout California also enabled the development of more land for agriculture. Fortunes were made in real estate, inventions in transportation and irrigation, and auxiliary businesses that were spurred by the expansion

of towns and cities. Victorian mansions popped up along prominent streets of new towns throughout the state.

After 1849, speculators, investors, and entrepreneurs made fortunes, the result of luck and cleverness. One of the fortune seekers was George Hearst, who left Missouri in 1850 after he had become convinced that there had been a gold strike in California. With some background and experience in mining, he spent almost ten years prospecting in quartz mines. In 1859, he rushed to Comstock, Nevada, when he had heard of a silver strike, and he acquired a small share in an untapped mine. That would be his introduction to the Comstock Lode and the genesis of his fortune. The Comstock Lode produced $400 million worth of silver and gold from 1859 through the late 1880s. Hearst and his partners also invested in mines in South Dakota, Utah, and Montana.

George and his wife, Phoebe Apperson Hearst, lived social lives in San Francisco. In 1874, when her son William Randolph was ten years old, Phoebe took him to Europe, where they traveled widely and he learned to appreciate different cultures and their art and architecture. George became a U.S. senator in 1887, and he and Phoebe moved to Washington, D.C.

When George died suddenly in 1891, Phoebe returned to California and managed the fortune. She became active in promoting progressive causes such as the education of women and children and made substantial contributions to the University of California at Berkeley throughout her lifetime, beginning with the establishment of a women's scholarship fund. While she was deeply involved in social issues, she also helped furnish her son William Randolph's new residence in San Simeon. Phoebe knew architect Julia Morgan and referred her for the project. For an even more unusual project, Phoebe hired Berkeley architect Bernard Maybeck to design a retreat in the style of a medieval castle/whimsical village on the Russian River, which was built from 1931 to 1942. After the fantastical house known as Wyntoon burned down, she hired Morgan, who had studied under and once worked for Maybeck, to rebuild it. The house is still owned by the Hearst family and maintained as a private residence.

Bernard Maybeck was trained at the École des Beaux-Arts in Paris from 1882 to 1886 and came to California in 1890. Two years later, he and his wife bought a house in Berkeley, a region with which he would forever be associated. In 1894, he joined the faculty of the University of California at Berkeley and taught drawing in the Civil Engineering College, establishing the College of Architecture for which he served as its first professor of architecture from 1889 to 1903. He would later collaborate on projects with one of his former students, Julia Morgan. Two of his notable commissions include the California Building for the 1893 World's Columbian Exposition in Chicago and the iconic San Francisco Palace of Fine Arts for the 1915 Panama–Pacific International Exposition. He was recognized as a major proponent of the Arts and Crafts movement's philosophy. His unique interpretation of design based on fine handcraftsmanship and the use of natural materials often combined a medieval architectural vocabulary with the most advanced technology. A group of residences he designed for his family and friends in the Berkeley hills represent his ideal of living in harmony with nature. Maybeck's domestic architecture and his First Church of Christ, Scientist, in Berkeley, epitomize his ability to use natural materials for elaborate carved, painted, and gilded wooden ornamentation.

During the era of the Gold Rush, fortunes were often made not by prospectors but by merchants who supplied them with dry goods, equipment, and food. Four such successful merchants, Leland Stanford, Collis P. Huntington, Mark Hopkins, and Charles F. Crocker, invested their money where they saw a tremendous and timely opportunity in the expansion of a railroad over the Sierra Nevadas and its connection to an eastern line. The "Associates," as they were called, would change the economy and culture of California and America when their Southern Pacific Railroad was linked to the Union Pacific Railroad in 1869, forming the first transcontinental railroad. These men dominated California's transportation industry for decades. With their fortunes, they built prestigious mansions in San Francisco and Sacramento, sparing no expense in hiring the most prominent architects and furnishing their residences with antique treasures from Europe and the Far East.

First-generation wealth also funded the lavish lifestyles of a second generation, who had learned to spend conspicuously. Theirs are some of the grandest houses built in California, from the time of the Gold Rush through the 1930s.

Multimillionaires such as Henry E. Huntington, heir to a third of his uncle Collis P. Huntington's fortune, parlayed their money into even greater riches. Huntington would move to Southern California in 1901 and make second and third fortunes by creating an interconnecting system of trolley car lines and in real estate development. His mansion in San Marino was built by the leading Pasadena architect of that time, Myron Hunt. Hunt, who was trained in the architectural program at M.I.T., adopted the Beaux-Arts tradition for his classically inspired Italianate villa for Huntington, as well as for the many commercial buildings he built in Pasadena.

Charles Templeton Crocker, grandson of railroad magnate Charles F. Crocker and heir to $5 million when he was 14, was educated at Yale, but he would return to the West and later build two spectacular homes, one in Hillsborough and another in Pebble Beach in 1911 and 1928 respectively. His 35,000-square-foot Uplands mansion in suburban Hillsborough was designed by leading San Francisco architect Willis Polk. It is now a private school. The Pebble Beach house is the only example of Byzantine-style architecture in America. It was designed by the illustrious Santa Barbara architect George Washington Smith in the latter part of his career.

Burrage Mansion, Redlands, Charles Brigham, designing architect, Charles C. Coveney, managing architect, Mission Revival style, 1901.

William Bowers Bourn II also used his inherited business to create further riches. William Bowers Bourn, Sr., owned the Empire Mine in Grass Valley. After his death in 1874, his wife managed the gold mine and other investments. When her 21-year-old son, William B. Bourn II, returned from Cambridge University in 1878 to take over operation of the failing mine, he reorganized investors and ran the mine under a new company. In 1881, he hired his cousin, George Starr, who had experience as a mining engineer, and in 1883 struck a vein of ore that proved even greater than the original find.

The Empire Mine became the most lucrative gold mine in California history. Bourn hired architect Willis J. Polk, a family friend, to design a brick-and-stone townhouse in San Francisco, as well as the family's large country house, Filoli, in Woodside. Bourn, along with many of the wealthy in San Francisco, built large estates in the exclusive enclaves of Hillsborough, Burlingame, Woodside, and other areas along the Peninsula after the 1906 earthquake.

Willis Polk also managed the construction of Carolands, an impressive French château-style residence built in Hillsborough for heiress Harriet Pullman Carolan. Her father, George Pullman, had founded the Pullman Palace Car Company, which produced luxury railway cars. Harriet and her husband, sportsman Francis Carolan, entertained often and lived lavishly as part of San Francisco's elite society crowd. Harriet's fortune was spent building Carolands and furnishing it with antiques she acquired abroad, mainly in France. Her inheritance was not sustainable and proved insufficient in maintaining the grand house on the large estate. She eventually sold Carolands, and its five hundred acres were subdivided.

When William Randolph Hearst inherited the family's ranchlands at San Simeon, he hired Julia Morgan to design a retreat on the mountaintop. Hearst Castle, also known as San Simeon, was the result. It is one of the best known American country houses in the world and visited by millions every year. Hearst's compound, which includes Casa Grande and three separate guest houses, represents Morgan's interpretation of Italian Renaissance– and Spanish Colonial–style architecture, modified with suggestions by a meticulous Hearst. He conferred and corresponded with Morgan on every detail of the design, both before and after he moved into the residence. With his inheritance, he acquired massive collections of now priceless European art and antique furnishings. One of his main goals in building the residence was to make an appropriate setting in which to display his treasures. Morgan understood this and ably completed the task. Hearst Castle became the delight and obsession of its owner. It was from this home that the tycoon ran his media empire.

Julia Morgan earned the first certificates ever awarded to a woman from the University of California at Berkeley's College of Engineering and L'École des Beaux-Arts in Paris (1896–1902). The buildings she designed in San Francisco withstood the 1906 earthquake, attesting to her engineering skills. Her designs also reflected her artistic talent and mastery of classical architecture. She maintained an office in San Francisco from 1904 to 1951, closing her doors at age 79, having built over 700 structures. While working for Hearst, she commuted by train between San Francisco and the site at San Simeon almost every weekend for 28 years in order to supervise the workers.

After the completion of the first transcontinental railroad in May 1869 and California's subsequent promotion in pamphlets during the 1870s as the perfect place to live, the state became a mecca of resorts. Grand luxury hotels were built by Southern Pacific Railroad Company executives and other companies to lure wealthy patrons from the Midwest and East Coast. Families would travel in luxurious Pullman railway cars to winter in such establishments as the Hotel del Monte in Pebble Beach, the Potter and Arlington hotels in Santa Barbara, and the Hotel del Coronado in San Diego. Upon experiencing the sunny, temperate weather, many of these visitors would return to build elegant first or second residences on large estates in these locales.

Areas such as Montecito, near Santa Barbara, were developed with grand European-style mansions and gardens, designs already familiar to their owners. Men who had risen to the top of their industries, such as Union Carbide Company cofounders C. K. G. Billings and George Owen Knapp and Chicago industrialist George Fox Steedman, retired from their hectic schedules to enjoy the good life in Montecito. Steedman hired George Washington Smith, the leading architect active in Santa Barbara during the 1920s. Social peers of Smith became his clientele, and for them he built striking homes, the designs of which were based on the vernacular farmhouses of southern Spain. His architectural practice flourished after 1918 and he is credited with bringing the Spanish Revival and Spanish Colonial Revival styles into prominence in Santa Barbara.

Dilettante architect and landscape designer Francis T. Underhill, who had moved to Santa Barbara and married into the first family of the town, the De la Guerras, designed elegant mansions that showed his affinity for classical motifs. Both Billings and Knapp hired him to build their mansions and he consulted with landscape designer Lockwood de Forest, Jr. on the gardens at Steedman's *Casa del Herrero* estate. When C. K. G. Billings's estate was ruined in the 1925 earthquake, the owners hired New York architect Carleton Monroe Winslow, who had worked on the plan of Balboa Park for the 1915 Panama–California Exposition in San Diego, to design a new hilltop residence and nearby guest houses.

Pasadena, San Marino, and Altadena became popular Southern California destinations to which the wealthy also flocked. The land boom of the 1880s created a swift populating of Southern California and made fortunes for real estate develop-

Earle C. Anthony House, Beverly Hills,
Bernard Maybeck, architect, Medieval
Revival style, 1927.

ers. The boom was the result of the railroads offering competitively priced tickets from the Midwest to Los Angeles in hopes of drawing people permanently to the land of sunshine. It worked. But by the 1890s, the boom was bust, and real estate sales subsided. Around this same time, many talented, formally trained architects had moved west for the opportunities afforded by these growing cities. The Southern California landscape was ultimately changed by the exceptional work of architects Myron

Hunt, Elmer Grey, Reginald D. Johnson, Gordon Kaufmann, Roland E. Coate, Sr., Irving Gill, Charles and Henry Greene, and others.

Charles and Henry Greene moved to Pasadena to be with their parents, who had relocated to California for their health. The brothers, who had studied architecture at M.I.T., opened their office in Pasadena and by 1902 were beginning to develop a distinctive style within the Arts and Crafts genre.

Their domestic designs evolved in sophistication from that point onward. During their most prolific period, from 1905 until 1911, they created a series of masterpieces that became known as ultimate bungalows. The Blacker House, well known as one of the Greenes' most brilliant compositions, was designed with an emphatic Far Eastern aesthetic guided by the Arts and Crafts dictum to use natural materials treated with artisan craftsmanship. This house embodies a masterful melding of design elements from China and Japan, evidenced in the finely carved exotic woods, hand-wrought iron and colorful art-glass lighting fixtures, glazed-tile decoration, and ornamental stylized gilt accents. Future houses designed by the Greene brothers would similarly reveal a keen understanding and love of Japanese design elements that would become their signature interpretation of the Arts and Crafts style.

With a virtual flood of people to Northern California during the Gold Rush, San Francisco arose overnight. The highly stylized Victorian architecture that we value today is the result of a confluence of trained architects, an endless supply of redwood from Humboldt County, and new inventions, such as the power sawmill and the jigsaw. Ornate mansions designed by such architectural luminaries as Willis J. Polk, Walter Bliss, William Faville, and others practicing in the Beaux-Arts tradition defined a sophisticated, elegant San Francisco.

In Southern California, the interconnecting railway and trolley car systems spurred development. Young architects who had recently finished their formal architectural training headed west to the land of opportunity. They settled in picturesque areas edged by the snow-capped San Gabriel Mountains or the Pacific Ocean and created an architecture still emulated today. A new aesthetic, one that reflected California's historic, Mediterranean-flavored past and responded to its ideal weather with patios, terraced gardens, and refreshing fountains, became the standard and remains that today.

Leland Stanford Mansion

Leland Stanford Mansion State Historic Park
Sacramento, 1857
Seth Babson, architect

*I*n 1861, while he was the Republican candidate for governor of California, Leland Stanford bought an elegant two-story house that had been built for wealthy businessman Shelton C. Fogus and was conveniently located just two blocks from where construction on the state Capitol building had commenced the year before. During his two-year term as governor (1862–1863), Stanford lived in the downtown house, where he also maintained his gubernatorial office. In 1872, the Stanfords completed an extensive remodeling that enlarged the house from 3,200 to 19,186 square feet and from two to four stories, crowning the magnificent Victorian mansion with a Second Empire mansard roof. They celebrated the occasion with a ball and reception for 700 guests. In 1873, the headquarters of the Central Pacific Railroad moved to San Francisco. Although the Stanfords relocated to San Francisco in 1874 and began construction on their Nob Hill mansion, which was completed in 1876, they continued to maintain and visit the Sacramento house. During his remarkable life, Stanford, who had been a lawyer and successful grocery merchant in his earlier years, became one of the most powerful and wealthy men in California. He and business partners Collis P. Huntington, Mark Hopkins, and Charles F. Crocker were collectively known as the Big Four. Their incorporation of the Central Pacific Railroad and successful commandeering of the completion of the first transcontinental railroad in America in 1869 had not only made them rich but had also given them dominance over Cali-

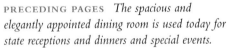

PRECEDING PAGES *The spacious and elegantly appointed dining room is used today for state receptions and dinners and special events.*

ABOVE *Main entrance doors of heavy, carved mahogany along with the complementary design of the banisters and newel post of the main staircase create an immediate impression of wealth for the former governor's home.*

ABOVE RIGHT *The centerpiece of the music room is the Stanfords' piano, which is original to the house. The room could be closed off for entertaining.*

OPPOSITE *The interiors were restored and recreated during the fourteen-year, $22 million rehabilitation to reflect décor found in 1872 photographs. An original marble fireplace surround and deeply saturated fabric colors set a tone of formal elegance for the family library.*

FOLLOWING PAGES *This re-created double parlor constitutes the heart of the main floor. The room's lavish decorative finishes of gilding on the carved wood elements and the shimmering blue damask upholstery create an atmosphere of luxury and opulence.*

ABOVE *The steep main staircase rises from the ground floor to the fourth floor.*

OPPOSITE *In the master bedroom on the third floor, a high ceiling and dark Victorian furnishings give the room formality, while several tall windows create spaciousness and let in much-welcomed light.*

1872: Remodel by Turton & Knox, contractors and builders

2005: Restoration and renovation by Page & Turnbull, architects

National Historic Landmark

California Historical Landmark

Owned by the State of California; administered by the California Department of Parks & Recreation

The restored mansion at the Stanford Mansion State Historic Park is open to the public.

fornia's transportation industry, which drove the development of the state's other industries and the growth of its towns and cities. Stanford would also become a U.S. senator, serving from 1885 until his death in 1893. He amassed a fortune that included more than 100,000 acres of vineyards and a horse breeding farm. In his later years, having become aware that his fortune could be used for the greater good of society, Stanford and his wife Jane built a university on their 8,800-acre Palo Alto stock farm to memorialize their only son, Leland, Jr., who had died in 1884 at the age of 15. To ensure its success they endowed Stanford University, which opened its doors in 1891, with $20 million.

After Senator Stanford's death, his widow remained active as the sole trustee of Stanford University, and she became its financial savior. Although Jane lived in their home on university grounds, she continued to maintain the Sacramento mansion until 1900, whereupon she donated it for use as an orphanage. Later it became a home for girls. In 1978, it was purchased by the State of California and designated a State Historic Park. Eventually, with private financing administered by the Leland Stanford Mansion Foundation and money secured from a state park bond act, the house and gardens underwent a $22 million restoration and rehabilitation that was completed in 2005. Today, even in the midst of its modern, urban setting, the spectacular mansion exudes an eloquent dignity and shines with exuberant Victorian beauty. It is the official site for grand government events and still features a private office for the governor of California.

*I*saac George Waterman Estate
Mira Vista

Montecito, 1892

PRECEDING PAGES *Mira Vista, the first of Montecito's grand estates, was built with locally quarried sandstone and landscaped with a series of terraced gardens. The garden facade's 45-foot-wide upper terrace has always been the perfect site for peaceful contemplation or convivial social events.*

LEFT *In 1913, architect Albert W. Pattiani designed the stone east wing of the house. At the same time, the west wing was remodeled to match the new three-story addition.*

OPPOSITE *On the main floor of the east wing, a paneled library's many sets of French doors open out onto the upper terrace and gardens. The room's restored floor is an intricate parquet design of Douglas fir and oak.*

oday, the great estate houses of Montecito that were built during the 1910s and 1920s are treasured for their historic significance and beautiful designs. But prior to that era, from the 1870s through the 1890s, Montecito was an agricultural region where settlers, lured by its mild climate and fertile soil, built homesteads, usually wooden Victorian-style houses, in the midst of large plots of farmed land. Horticulturalists also realized the potential in the perfect growing conditions and planted experimental gardens and nurseries. But no one had yet developed an estate that included a grand house and formal landscaping that could be considered a showplace.

Mira Vista became that first celebrated estate. In 1892, the 21-year-old musician Isaac George Waterman, heir to a Pennsylvania iron and coal fortune, and his wife moved onto 25 acres in Montecito, and began to build impressive stone additions to the existing wood-frame house. A grand music room, where they could host recitals that included performances by them on flute and piano, was attached to a two-story tower. Waterman spent extravagantly and landscaped the estate with elegant terraced gardens that led to an expansive lemon orchard lined with canary palm trees. The magnificent estate became a well-known local feature.

By 1905, when Waterman sold *Mira Vista*, it had grown to a landscaped estate of 42 acres. William Griffith Henshaw, a San Francisco developer and engineer, purchased it in 1913 and hired architect Albert W. Pattiani to remodel and design additions that remain

visible today. A three-story tower of rough-hewn sandstone was built to replace the wood-frame house. An existing tower, situated on the west side of the house, was remodeled to match the new one. A 50-foot loggia was added above the music room. The now even grander *Mira Vista* estate, with its luscious gardens and 45-foot-wide terrace, saw more extravagant entertaining and increased fame.

After its sale as part of the Henshaw estate in 1945, *Mira Vista* was bought and used as a college dormitory, eventually falling into ruin under subsequent private ownership.

When the Gale family purchased the house, along with two and a half additional acres, in 1993, the estate had been neglected for more than twenty years and was almost beyond repair. But the family had fallen in love with the historic property, a fortuitous synchronicity of the right persons at the right time being in the right place. "Loving takes responsibility," Mrs. Gale believes, so with enthusiasm, passion, and vision, she took the lead in a commitment to restore and remodel the dilapidated house, ever cognizant of honoring the estate's significant history. Los Angeles contractor Robert Glaus collaborated with her on the implementation of design concepts and the meticulous two-year renovation.

Today, the house shines as one of the finest stone structures in and around Santa Barbara. Its replanted gardens thrive in the Mediterranean climate, and the magnificent estate has been brought gloriously back to the future.

ABOVE AND OPPOSITE
The Gales transformed the original music room into a light-filled living room and an adjacent two-story dining room, separated from the larger room by classical columns. New decorative wrought iron embellishes the balcony.

FOLLOWING PAGES
The south facade contains what is now the main entrance. The restoration of the fifty-foot-long rooftop loggia above the living room has created more space for enjoying the outdoors.

1892: Music room, west tower, various outbuildings built by owner Isaac G. Waterman

1915: Remodel and addition of third story to west wing; additions of loggia, east wing, superintendent's house, and gatehouse:
Albert W. Pattiani, architect

1995: Renovation and remodel by Tina Gale, designer, and Robert Glaus, contractor/design consultant

Harry M. and Lillie Spreckels Holbrook Mansion

San Francisco, 1905

Walter D. Bliss, Bliss & Faville, architects

Photographed by Paul Rocheleau

T

ohn and Paula Murphy own a magnificent, meticulously restored San Francisco townhouse mansion built in 1905 in the style of a French château. The Murphys acquired the house in 1997 and allowed it to be used as the venue for the San Francisco University High School Decorator Showcase, an event that raised more than $500,000 for minority scholarship funds. To prepare it as their residence, the Murphys thoroughly renovated and remodeled the five-level residence to give it a cohesive interior design worthy of its sophisticated Beaux-Arts exterior.

The Pacific Heights residential area of San Francisco began to flourish after a cable-car system linked it to the downtown financial district in the late nineteenth century. Soon thereafter, the wealthy claimed lots and built mansions that took advantage of the spectacular views of the Bay. John D. Spreckels, heir to the Spreckels sugar fortune, built a large family home and purchased nearby lots for family members. A lengthy article in the society section of the *San Francisco Call* announced that Lillian ("Lillie") Carolyn had been married on February 26, 1905, to Harry Morgan Holbrook, owner of a manufacturing firm with offices in San Francisco, Sacramento, Los Angeles, and New York, at her parents' home on Pacific Avenue.

The wealthy society couple chose the architectural firm of Bliss & Faville to design a French Provincial–style mansion. Walter Bliss and William Faville had studied architecture

together at M.I.T., the first American university to offer a Beaux-Arts curriculum in 1893. After leaving M.I.T. in 1895, they secured positions in the offices of McKim, Mead & White, the preeminent architectural firm working in the Beaux-Arts genre in the United States. The two men subsequently opened their San Francisco office in 1898, quickly becoming the most prolific and prominent architects in the city. True to the tradition of Beaux-Arts classicism, their domestic and commercial architecture embodied classical beauty with formal, ornately embellished,

OPPOSITE *A Carrara marble formal entry stairway accented with architectural landscaping leads to an enclosed vestibule for the grand foyer entry. Doors are framed in ornate handwrought ironwork.*

RIGHT *Entry to the private library/clubroom through a gilded and paneled hall becomes even more elegant with the architectural accent of a coffered and barrel-vaulted ceiling.*

elegant designs. Among their many famous buildings now designated as city landmarks are the Bank of California, the Geary Theater and Annex, and the Security Pacific Bank.

Another contributor to the original grandeur of the Murphys'
townhouse mansion was architect Albert L. Farr, who designed
prestigious homes throughout the Bay area. His extensive remodeling work on the house in 1930 included the addition of a clubroom with a concealed bar and large solariums affording Bay
views from the dining room and master bedroom.

The expert work the Murphys undertook in 1997 brought their
historic home up to the highest standards for contemporary living

ABOVE *The breakfast room/solarium,
with its twelve-foot ceiling and fine
architectural moldings, affords spectacular
views of San Francisco Bay.*

OPPOSITE *In the dramatic hunter green
and gold-gilt-trimmed dining room, a
massive French mahogany dining table
can seat twenty-four guests.*

RIGHT *The main bedroom suite includes a master bedroom, for which the striking royal blue damask upholstered wall treatment creates high drama, and spacious and luxuriously appointed his and hers en-suite master bathrooms created by architect Jorge de Quesada.*

FOLLOWING PAGES *The formality of an intimate enclosed garden in the back that features boxwood parterres complements the Beaux-Arts townhouse mansion.*

while also ensuring its longevity as one of San Francisco's truly singular properties. The spacious entry foyer with an impressive cascading staircase introduces the formal salon, which is marked by a twelve-foot-high gilded ceiling. The dramatic dining room, whose massive French mahogany table seats 24, also sparkles with gilded accents. An atmosphere of graciousness pervades the beloved home. Prior additions made by the Schwabacher family in 1930, in addition to those undertaken by the Murphys in 1997, blend with the century-old architecture to enhance the living spaces and highlight the panoramic views of the San Francisco Bay and the Golden Gate Bridge.

1930: Remodel by Albert L. Farr, Farr & Ward, architects

1972: Remodel

1997: Remodel of master bathroom suite by Jorge de Quesada, architect; remodel of guest bathrooms, writer's atelier, home office, and Bay-view windows by Dan Phipps, architect; remodel of kitchen, pantry, and library/media room by Barbara Scavullo Design

Residence of John and Paula Murphy

Robert R. Blacker House

San Marino, 1907

Charles Greene and Henry Greene, architects

PRECEDING PAGES
The magnificent Greene and Greene–designed Blacker House, built in 1907 as the centerpiece of the Oak Knoll development in Pasadena, is prominently sited on a corner with an expansive front lawn.

LEFT *The Mission-style entry porch has a low roof and broad-hooded art glass lanterns that shed a glowing light and lead to a welcoming bank of tripartite doors at the entrance.*

OPPOSITE *The Greenes created a dramatic entrance angled off the side of the house, with a motor court and a porte cochere that features an anchor pier of irregular clinker bricks, an oversized broad-hooded art glass and brass lantern, and open-timber trusses of hefty wooden beams carved with a distinctive silhouette.*

In 1907, architects Charles and Henry Greene designed an impressive finely crafted wood-and-brick residence for, appropriately, the retired lumber-and-brick baron Robert Roe Blacker and his wife, Nellie. It was to be situated on a large corner lot in Pasadena's Oak Knoll subdivision. In 1906, the landscape architect Frederick Law Olmsted devised a comprehensive plan for the former Oak Knoll Ranch, taking care to make the best use of the terrain's gently rolling hills. The Blacker House would become the area's centerpiece. The property had included a large lily pond, a carriage house/garage, a caretaker's cottage, and extensive gardens of exotic plants. Although the original five acres have since been subdivided, a sprawling front lawn serves as a majestic setting for the bold, beautiful architecture, giving the house a prominence amid the landscaped gardens and towering trees, complete with a picturesque backdrop of the San Gabriel Mountains.

The Blacker House is regarded as one of the Greenes' most brilliant compositions. Its design was guided by the Arts and Crafts dictum to use natural materials treated with artisan craftsmanship. The house's interiors masterfully meld design elements from China and Japan, such as finely carved exotic woods, copper and colorful art glass lighting fixtures, glazed tile decoration, and ornamental stylized gilt accents.

It might be said that the house's proportions, exterior details, and interior finishes and ornamentation are perfect. Upon entering a spacious, majestic central reception area, a

visitor is made immediately aware of how the magnificent house unfolds, with first-floor public rooms situated on either side and views from the back terrace to the gardens. A wide, graceful staircase, with a landing from which to enjoy the golden light streaming in from large decorative windows, leads to a second story. At this level are private living quarters that include bedrooms, bathrooms, and a sleeping porch, now enclosed.

After the death of Nellie Blacker in 1946, the Blacker House changed ownership a number of times and had been neglected to such an extent that by the time the current owners purchased the residence in 1994, it needed extensive work. In addition, all but three of the original handcrafted lighting fixtures and most of the

ABOVE *The graceful design for the main hall or central reception area features softly finished teak wall paneling, a ceiling of Douglas fir heavy-timber construction with panels of Port Orford cedar between the beams, and five hanging lanterns that cast a warm glow.*

OPPOSITE *Northern light illuminates the nature-inspired imagery in the leaded-and-stained-glass bay window at the landing of the main stairway.*

FOLLOWING PAGES *A large dining area is composed of a dining room and a sunny breakfast room that has three walls of floor-to-ceiling windows. A painted frieze encircles the rooms and decorates the space above the central beam. Light trays are suspended over each of the two dining tables on leather straps with wood rings.*

ABOVE *In the living room, a frieze and corner ceiling detail features a gesso bas-relief lotus-leaf pattern covered in gold leaf muted with a surface glazing. Light from six art glass hanging lanterns reflects the gold in the frieze and washes the room in a subtle warm glow.*

OPPOSITE *The living room fireplace surround was designed in Grueby tiles. The fender is crafted of sheet brass with a copper-brown patina and features a folded-ribbon design. The three-part, hinged, folding fire screen's bronze frame is detailed with imagery from plants, as is the bas-relief of the lower inset panels in brass and copper.*

RIGHT *Carved details of the velvety smooth teak beams in the main hall, such as the shaping at the ends of the heavy beams and the corbel design on the stairway column, emphasize the subtle Oriental theme of the house.*

art glass installations had been removed in 1985 and sold at auction. As part of a thorough five-year restoration and renovation, the current owners had the missing light fixtures duplicated by skilled artisans and many of the original furnishings reproduced by master craftsman James M. Ipekjian. Shop drawings and archival photographs from the Greenes' workshop, along with examination of original pieces in museums and private collections, were used to achieve a historical authenticity.

The owners' passion and consideration for exacting details has produced a renovation worthy of this extraordinary work of art. The house's original soothing, majestic beauty has been realized through a monumental preservation effort, directed by owners whose thoughtfulness, thoroughness, and care have saved this important piece of the world's architectural heritage. The Blacker House is now a gleaming jewel among the extant Greene and Greene houses.

RIGHT *A series of decoratively carved French doors opens from the main hall onto the back porch, affording wide views of the garden. Above each door, an iridescent art glass window lets colored light into the large interior space.*

FOLLOWING PAGES *At the rear of the house, a kitchen herb and vegetable garden and roses under a wooden trellis add to the charm of the grand Arts and Crafts masterpiece.*

2000 (and ongoing): Restoration by Randell L. Makinson, architect

Listed on the National Register of Historic Places

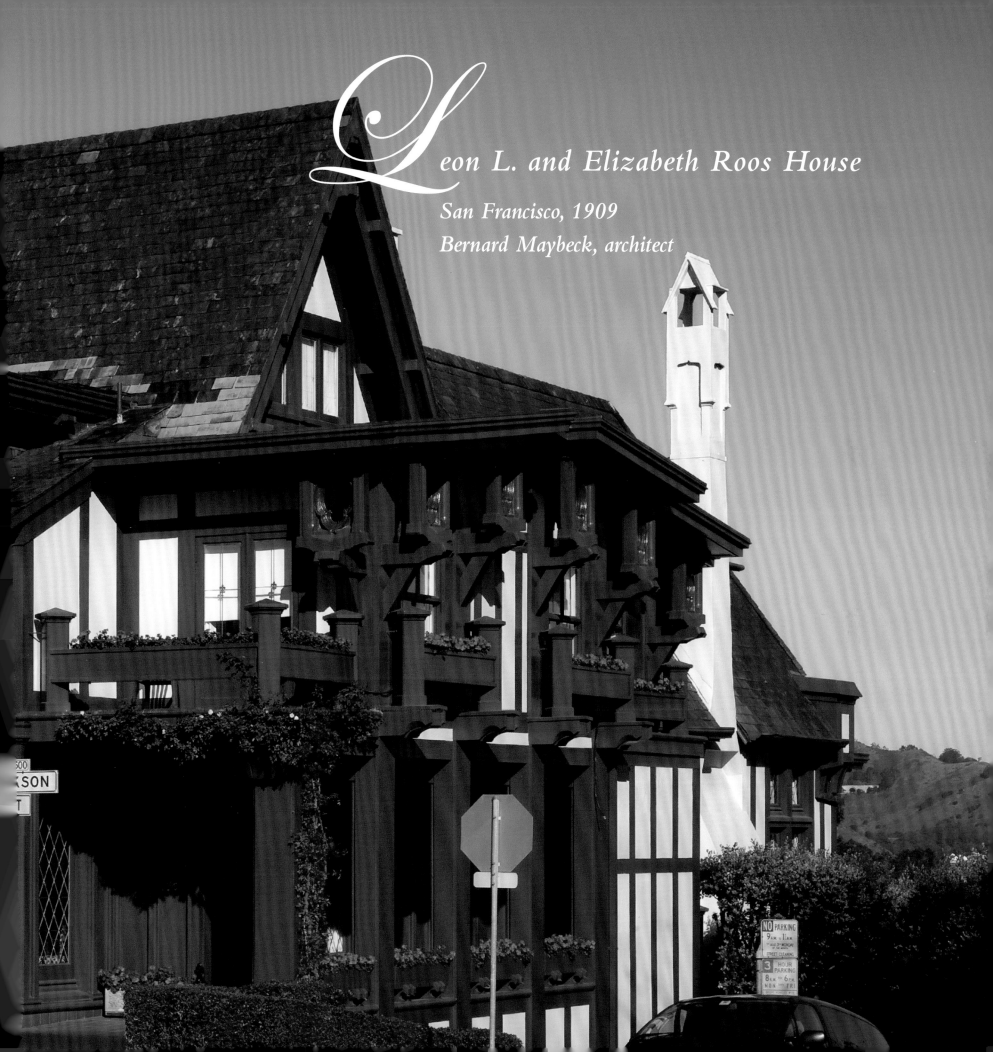

Leon L. and Elizabeth Roos House

San Francisco, 1909
Bernard Maybeck, architect

*T*he downtown San Francisco mansion that architect Bernard Maybeck designed for newly-weds Leon L. and Elizabeth Leslie Roos in 1909 fulfilled the bride's wish for a house with a decidedly theatrical flair. Maybeck had a love of the medieval and an affinity for theater and drama, often dressing at home in eccentric period costumes and performing plays with his family. He was the perfect architect for the job. His vision for dramatic architecture combined whimsical elements with grand statements and practical solutions with fanciful treatments. The interior of this immense residence is welcoming as well as awe-inspiring. Even the impressive, voluminous living room exudes warmth and intimacy with its exciting design.

The living room in the Roos House is Maybeck's interpretation of a medieval baronial great hall, and there is a visceral pleasure one feels while in it. Metallic threads embroidered on the velvet upholstery flicker in the afternoon light, and exotic glass pendant lights glow at dusk, evoking an atmosphere of centuries past. Furthermore, the warm redwood paneling and immense hearth and mantelpiece, work to create a cohesive vision and luxurious design that is a thrill to experience.

Maybeck cleverly disguised the enormity of the house with a highly ornamented exterior, as well as with the arrangement of the different masses on the sharply sloping hillside lot and a variety of rooflines. Tudor-style half-timbering on the stucco surface imbues the exterior with a vertical orientation. Dormers and balconies built with heavy wood mem-

LEFT   *The front doors are painted with a striking glossy red.*

OPPOSITE   *The entry foyer between the great room and the dining room has a well-designed skylight and doors paneled with antique amethyst velvet. A medieval chair is part of the owner's collection.*

FOLLOWING PAGES
The great hall has original Maybeck-designed furnishings, a series of clustered pendant lights, and a monolithic floor to ceiling stonelike fireplace and chimney plate.

86–87   *A pair of early carved walnut armchairs are displayed at the far end of the entry foyer where a door leads to the raised library/sitting area facing the great room.*

bers, wide eaves, and charming decorative features with pops of color (bright red geraniums in window boxes and carved wooden balconies with quatrefoils painted red) mitigate the massiveness and horizontality of the structure. A protected side entry belies the magnificence inside.

The daughter-in-law of the original owners and her husband, who conducted at the San Francisco Ballet for 14 years, currently reside in the lovingly maintained historic house. It is space well used; grandchildren and other members of the family fill the house on holidays and special occasions. As the original owners shared their love of the theater and music, so do the current owners continue the tradition by hosting intimate musical evenings and gatherings for organizations. In this glorious space, the owners have held such events as a ballet performance accompanied by piano and cello as a benefit for Lysée Française, recitals by the San Francisco Contemporary Music Players, a chamber symphony founded by the owner over 40 years ago, and parties to benefit the San Francisco Museum and Historical Society. Such gatherings allow guests to experience firsthand the rich ambience of the great living room.

TOP LEFT *Unusual lighting in the house includes small pendant lights in the upstairs study created by Maybeck with silk and beads.*

BOTTOM LEFT *In the dining room, decorative metalwork includes heavily perforated helmetlike sconces and an ornate escutcheon plate.*

RIGHT *A small paneled library off of the great room is raised with shallow steps to become a private sitting area.*

FOLLOWING PAGES
LEFT *The fireplace surround in the upstairs study is polychromed with Renaissance detail. The ornate andirons are original to the house.*

MIDDLE *Dominating the great room and giving it a medieval sensibility is a large fireplace surround and floor-to-ceiling chimney plate composed of cast plaster and tinted cement that mimics elaborately carved stone.*

RIGHT *The dining room's cast-iron fireplace surround and andirons are a substantive element in the well-lit room.*

PAGES 92–93 *Leaded-glass windows, which follow a theme of English cottage architecture, let much-needed light into the wood-paneled dining room.*

Alterations: 1913, living room; 1916, garage added; 1919, dressing rooms added; 1926, second floor study added; all by Bernard Maybeck, architect

San Francisco Historic Landmark

*D*avid B. Gamble House

Pasadena, 1907–09
Charles Greene and Henry Greene, architects

One of the best known, indeed iconic, houses designed by Pasadena architects Charles and Henry Greene is the residence they built from 1907 to 1909 for David and Mary Gamble and their family. Gamble had retired from his executive position at the Procter & Gamble Company in Cincinnati, Ohio, when he hired the Greene brothers to design his winter home in California. The Greenes were at the height of their careers when they began studies for the house.

In 1966, the Gamble heirs deeded the estate to the City of Pasadena, whereupon the property opened as a house museum, regularly enjoyed by the public and studied by scholars. It is the only Greene and Greene house that contains all of its original furniture, custom designed and built by Greene and Greene. This extraordinary Arts and Crafts masterpiece, one of a handful of Greene and Greene "ultimate bungalows," is the only example that can be experienced in its entirety, as it was intended for the family.

After the Greenes were first given the freedom to design the Tichenor House (1905) in Long Beach, their work qualitatively changed. The very scale of their projects increased, concomitant with the budgets of their clients, while the highly gifted woodworkers Peter and John Hall raised the level of artistry.

The Greenes were perfectionists. They sited their houses, almost all built in Southern California, in relation to the given landscape and designed according to the individual

ABOVE AND OPPOSITE *In the entry, fine craftsmanship is evident in Burmese teak and Honduran mahogany woodwork that was finished with a velvety surface, mortise-and-tenon joinery, and art glass designs that included references to nature, such as vines, trees, and birds.*

FOLLOWING PAGES *The house contains the original furnishings and is, therefore, the only one of the Greenes' masterpieces to be experienced in its entirety, as it was intended for the family. An abundance of seating areas are available in the living room.*

OPPOSITE *A built-in sideboard with drawers and cabinets of Honduran mahogany is the focal point in the dining room. Leaded and art glass windows above it bring nature in with a design of a flowering vine. The unique* tsuba *form of the table's surface is taken from the traditional Japanese sword-guard shape.*

RIGHT *In the living room, an inglenook provides privacy in front of the hearth. The fireplace-surround tiles are inset with a flower-and-vine motif specifically designed for the Gambles.*

ABOVE *A bureau of bird's-eye maple inlaid with silver and Indonesian vermilion wood and a matching chair reside in the guest bedroom off the entry hall. The wall sconce has a silver-inlaid mahogany bracket holding a leaded art glass shade with a pink rose design framed in mahogany.*

RIGHT *The hall is filled with light from glazed double doors that lead out to the back patio and gardens.*

OPPOSITE *An iridescent art glass window lets much-needed light into the back stairwell and the back hall and provides a touch of color to the surrounding wood paneling. A smaller window of textured obscure glass opens onto the linen closet.*

RIGHT *Even in the service zone of the house, the Greenes wed utility and beauty. The butler's pantry is fitted with two zinc-clad sinks, and all cabinetry, doors, and trim were designed in clear and bird's-eye maple.*

needs of the client. The architects used different decorative motifs carved in wood or designed as art glass to distinguish each house. For the Gamble House, they adopted representations of nature—vines, trees, and birds. To strengthen the structures, they used mortise-and-tenon joinery, wooden dowels, and specially designed wrought-iron straps. Their use of indigenous materials, such as arroyo rocks in some of the Pasadena houses, complemented the exteriors that they sheathed in stained-wood shingles. Exotic woods, such as Honduran mahogany and Burmese teak, finished with velvet-like surfaces defined the Gamble House interiors. Here and in other Greene and Greene residences are dramatic lighting fixtures of handworked copper or carved wood with colorful and/or iridescent glass, glazed-tile fireplace surrounds and hearths, custom-woven rugs, and intricate art glass window treatments.

The continued aesthetic appeal and respect for their work attests to Charles and Henry Greene's permanent and prominent place in America's architectural heritage.

LEFT *The house gives the impression that it is one with nature, its asymmetrical design oriented horizontally and sheathed in naturally stained wood. A halfellipse of lawn hides the brick driveway and creates a visual foundation for the structure.*

RIGHT *The Greenes' ambitious plan for the back terrace and garden landscaping included a Japanese-inspired pond bordered by a low clinker-brick wall with a series of arches.*

2004: Restoration by Kelly Sutherlin McLeod, AIA, restoration architect; Historic Resources Group, preservation consultants; Griswold Conservation Associates, architectural conservator

National Historic Landmark

California Historical Landmark

Listed on the National Register of Historic Places

Owned by the City of Pasadena

Administered by the University of Southern California School of Architecture in a joint agreement with the City of Pasadena

Henry E. Huntington Mansion

at The Huntington Library, Art Collections,
and Botanical Gardens
San Marino, 1911
Myron Hunt, Hunt & Grey, architects

PRECEDING PAGES
The 1911 Beaux-Arts mansion was designed by Pasadena architect Myron Hunt and incorporates the massive design and elaborate ornamentation of a sixteenth-century Italian villa.

LEFT   *The former Henry E. Huntington residence is now the Huntington Art Gallery, which displays a world-class collection of European art and is part of the Huntington Library, Art Collections, and Botanical Gardens, one of the finest collections-based research and educational centers in the world.*

OPPOSITE   *The architectural design for the east wing of the mansion incorporates a classically inspired loggia conceived by Huntington to be used as an "outdoor living room."*

The magnificent 55,000-square-foot Beaux-Arts Italianate villa, originally the San Marino residence of Henry E. Huntington and his wife, Arabella, is now the Huntington Art Gallery, which displays a world-class European art collection. Huntington intended that the house would one day become a public art gallery—and it opened as such in 1928, one year after his death. Today, the Huntington Library, Art Collections, and Botanical Gardens is one of the finest collections-based research and educational centers in the world.

Collis P. Huntington, a wealthy railroad magnate, had hired his industrious teenaged nephew, Henry, promoting him until, in 1892, the then 42-year-old was put in charge of the Southern Pacific Company at its headquarters in San Francisco. By then, the elder Huntington had become Henry's surrogate father, mentor, and friend. By the late 1890s, however, Henry was fatigued by the demands of the ever contentious railroad business just as his marriage was failing. In 1900, his beloved uncle died, leaving him one-third of an immense fortune ($50 million by today's standards). Collis's widow, Arabella, who was Henry's age, received two-thirds of the fortune. Thirteen years after Collis's death, Henry and Arabella, both 63, were married in 1913. Arabella was a sophisticated woman who spent lavishly on fine jewelry and had amassed an impressive collection of European art. After her marriage to Henry, she inspired him to begin establishing a collection of his own, which formed the core of the collection in the gallery today.

OPPOSITE AND RIGHT *The main floor contains a series of domestic period rooms that reflect their original early twentieth-century ambiance. Drawing rooms and the library are furnished with French gilded armchairs and settees upholstered with eighteenth-century tapestry, magnificent carpets from the Savonnerie manufactory, and tapestries from the series* The Noble Pastoral, 1757–1760, Beauvais Manufactory, *after cartoons by François Boucher.*

FOLLOWING PAGES *In the large oak-paneled library, spectacular French furnishings include a Louis XIV desk and table ornamented with ormolu detailing, two Savonnerie carpets designed for Louis XIV's redecoration of the Louvre palace, and tapestries such as* The Fountain of Love, *one of six eighteenth-century French tapestries from* The Noble Pastoral.

Henry had first visited the sprawling San Marino Ranch in 1892 en route to his new position in San Francisco. After his uncle's death, Henry divested himself of business in San Francisco, moved to Southern California, and in 1903 bought the 501-acre San Marino Ranch along with other properties nearby. He hired prominent Pasadena architect Myron Hunt to design his residence.

Hunt ultimately designed many buildings for Huntington, including the mansion, completed in 1911, the library, completed in 1920, and other important community buildings in Pasadena. In 1905, the young landscape gardener William Hertrich was asked to develop extensive gardens for the ranch. Among other insightful plans, he established a nursery in which to propagate the thousands of needed plants. The many botanical gardens, now fully mature, are world-renowned.

In his decision to move to Southern California, Henry was energized by a new vision for developing the greater Los Angeles area, taking advantage of the limitless opportunities for growth. He again found himself in the transportation business. His companies built the interurban transportation system that connected 50 communities along the coast, from Santa Monica to Balboa

PRECEDING PAGES *The Thornton Portrait Gallery is a 2,900-square-foot hall added in 1934. One of the most famous paintings in the collection is* The Blue Boy, *by Thomas Gainsborough, c. 1770.*

LEFT *Twenty-two thematic galleries on the second floor include those highlighting nineteenth-century British art and design, Renaissance paintings and sculpture, eighteenth-century French art, and with rooms displaying porcelain and silver.*

OPPOSITE *Classical architectural detailing that includes a series of fluted columns with Ionic capitals, dentil and other ornately carved trim work, and a coffered ceiling, creates formality and grandeur in the large east–west hall.*

RIGHT
Classically inspired sculpture is found throughout the gardens. To the west of the house, the carved columns of a seventeenth-century Italian stone and wrought-iron temple encircle the marble statue Cupid Blindfolding Youth, *1876.*

FOLLOWING PAGES
126–127 *A moon bridge and Japanese house are featured elements in the Japanese Garden, one of more than twelve themed gardens that cover 120 acres of the Huntington Botanical Gardens.*

128–129 *The Desert Garden features magnificent cacti and succulents.*

and inland from Redlands to Pasadena and the San Fernando Valley, and provided electricity for the trolleys and residential use. Furthermore, his companies administered the purchases of land where the transit lines were to be laid and the sale of the subdivided land. These investments produced another fortune and made him the most influential man in Southern California's swiftly changing economy.

Henry E. Huntington's legacy is not only the powerful and brilliant Southern California we see today, but also the sharing of his art collections, rare books, and manuscripts, and the vast and fascinating botanical gardens of his beloved estate. These latter gifts are for the enjoyment and education of scholars, scientists, and the public in perpetuity.

2008: Restoration by Bert England, Earl Corp., architect; Stephen Farneth, Architectural Resources Group, preservation architect

Frank C. Havens Estate, Wildwood

Oakland, 1911
Bernard Maybeck, architect

PRECEDING PAGES
*For Wildwood's design, architect
Bernard Maybeck cascaded four stories
down the steep hillside and oriented
large windows, a wide deck, and
terraces toward the south to take
advantage of the magnificent views
of the canyon and hills beyond.*

LEFT *Winding paths meander
through the lush landscape of the
terraced hillside gardens below
the house.*

OPPOSITE *Maybeck's design
for the main entrance is subdued
compared to the house's elaborate
interiors. Carved elements embellish
a substantial porte cochere that leads
to an entry vestibule.*

*I*n 1908, Frank Colton Havens, one of Oakland's most influential citizens, hired Berkeley architect Bernard Maybeck to design a large house on 55 acres of a small canyon in the recently incorporated Piedmont area of Oakland. Maybeck's design cascaded four stories down the steep hillside and oriented large windows, a wide deck, and terraces toward the south to take advantage of magnificent views of the canyon and hills beyond. The north elevation, however, belies the voluminous and opulent interior.

Havens was an extraordinary person. He left home when he was 16 and sailed from the East Coast around Cape Horn to California, Honolulu, and eventually China. It is assumed he acquired his love of the culture and architecture of the Far East while living there. He came to San Francisco at 21, and ten years later had become a successful stock-broker. He later formed investment companies, including a realty syndicate with holdings of 13,000 acres in the East Bay that made him an extremely wealthy man.

Devoted to improving Oakland as he developed its real estate, he consolidated an early transit system, created a state-of-the-art water system, planted over a million trees in the then sparsely wooded foothills, and built a public museum to house his European art collection. He was a visionary thinker whose literary friends included Jack London and poet George Sterling. Havens' wife, Lila, who had been his secretary and whom he married after his first wife had died, shared his love of Far East aesthetics. She was an active social

and civic leader. And as a devotee of yoga, she followed the teachings of Far Eastern philosophy and hosted gurus at her home.

The mansion had been described as a maharaja's palace in newspaper articles of the day that reported on the many lavish parties, festivals, and charity events the Havenses hosted. The house was renowned for its exotic interiors, where a generous use of satin-finished teak defined spacious stairwells and warm, enveloping rooms. An atmosphere of luxury was created with the introduction of unusual decorations that included walls lined with brilliant, colorful silk brocade, huge pendant lanterns of perforated, patterned copper or brass, and intricately carved teak furniture and ornamentation from India and China.

After Maybeck finished his work in 1911, it is believed that the Havenses hired Louis C. Tiffany, then in New York, to embellish the interior spaces. A probable completion date for the elegant interior design coincided with the opening of the 1915 Panama–Pacific International Exposition, for which it is reported the Havenses entertained extravagantly. It is likely that Tiffany's former business partner, Lockwood de Forest, Sr., was also involved. After a visit to India from 1881 to 1882, de Forest imported hand-carved and inlaid furniture from the misti workshops of Ahmedabad.

ABOVE *Throughout the house, often described as an Indian palace, brass pendant lanterns from India that feature ornate perforated designs create a low-lit, glowing interior that contributes to the exotic atmosphere.*

ABOVE RIGHT *The huge master bedroom features Huanghuali (Pte-tocarpus indicus), an exotic wood widely used throughout the Ming and Ch'ing dynasties (1368–1912) in China that is now extinct. Many golden-colored panels trimmed in the exotic wood conceal drawers, shelves, and closets that may be revealed with the touch of a button.*

OPPOSITE *Glazed porcelain Thai temple guardians from the Sukhothai Kingdom (1238–1438) from the owner's private collection and antique lacquered camphor wood columns guard the entry from the entrance hall into the Chinese sitting room, whose columns, walls, and ceiling were imported by the Tiffany Studio from China at the end of the Ch'ing Dynasty.*

ABOVE *Steps that go up the hillside or form a path that winds through the terraced gardens make the private backyard and enclosed Thai porch accessible. The Gujarati carved window boxes were imported from and are typical of eighteenth- and nineteenth-century Ahmedabad window boxes from Gujarat Province, India.*

RIGHT *Decorative ceilings of mica with carved wood overlays add to the opulence of the enclosed Thai porch and breakfast room.*

LEFT *The Japanese tea room, at the far east end of the house, is a glorious and serene space. Tatami mats cover the floor, and shoji screens may close off the rest of the house or open to a covered porch. The sleek design is complemented with ornately carved cantilevered benches and coffered ceilings that expand the sense of space.*

OPPOSITE *A black lacquer room with a lacquer-and-gold-leaf ceiling in the style of Tokugawa temples in Japan leads from the entrance hall into the Japanese (tatami) tea room.*

PRECEDING PAGES *In the 55-by-35-foot living room on one of the lower levels, a massive fireplace is framed with an ornately carved teakwood tree-of-life pattern. Also in the room is the extraordinary elephant table, the top of which measures eleven and a half feet long and over three feet wide. It was cut from a single piece of teak. The table is embellished with eighteen-inch-tall carved elephants.*

RIGHT *Original to the downstairs formal dining room are its carved octagonal table and set of matching chairs. The ceiling features indirect lighting through the topaz stones and amber cathedral-glass inset in an enormous carved teak lotus-blossom design. From a small landing and musicians' gallery that overlooks the dining room, a group of musicians may entertain guests seated below.*

De Forest became the designer of fashionable East India rooms for the millionaires of the Gilded Age. When de Forest dissolved his business around 1906, Tiffany bought his remaining inventory. Architectural historian Sally B. Woodbridge thinks it likely that de Forest, who had built a residence in Santa Barbara by 1915, may have been contracted to install some of the decorative pieces from his former inventory.

The current owner, an American who lived in China for thirty years, completed an extensive eight-year restoration in 2002 and honors the elegant historic interior with sensitive conservation, augmenting it with his own collection of beautiful Asian antiques.

1915: Remodel by Louis C. Tiffany, Tiffany and Company; Lockwood de Forest, Sr., designer

2002: Restoration, remodel, and seismic retrofitting

Guy Hyde Chick House

Oakland, 1915
Bernard Maybeck, architect

One normally doesn't think of houses designed by Berkeley architect Bernard Maybeck as modern architecture. Most of his early work heavily referenced medieval and Gothic styles. But the house that Maybeck designed from 1914 to 1915 for the Guy Hyde Chick family combines an unusual and charming exterior treatment immediately recognizable as that of Maybeck with a decidedly modern interior.

The house, built of wood, glass, and concrete, is set on a forested hillside of aged live oaks in a small Oakland canyon, a locale that is certainly picturesque but also extremely vulnerable to forest fires. In fact, the devastating conflagration of 1991 that destroyed 3,000 structures in the Berkeley and Oakland hills raged in this canyon. The house was thought to be lost. But when the owner returned to the burned site, he was flabbergasted to see his house miraculously unharmed.

Maybeck's design eludes categorization. The house is the work of one of the major champions of the Arts and Crafts philosophy and is therefore rooted in a connection to nature and the use of natural materials. It features, however, innovative stylized architectural details from a variety of idioms. Functional elements become works of art. For example, there is a substantial cast-cement pillar with projections that brace horizontal wood members that in turn support the wisteria-covered pergola over the curved patio and arched cove at the main south entrance. The whole form gives the effect of a tree, with a symbolic

PRECEDING PAGES *The house is designed with a fenestrated enfilade that stretches from the living room at one end of the house to the dining room at the other. In between these two main rooms are wide connecting hallways and the spacious entry foyer.*

LEFT *An unusual design element in the finely carved wooden banister is an urn shape that links the second floor to the staircase in the entry.*

OPPOSITE *A fireplace in the intimate library/study off the living room provides warmth.*

FOLLOWING PAGES *In the living room, an abundance of oversized plate-glass windows and nine-foot-tall glazed French doors create a sense of intimacy with the gracefully tangled oaks outside.*

trunk and limbs supporting an airy canopy. The house appears to be a work of nature.

Integrating the house with its natural surroundings was a paramount design concern. To draw the house further into its landscape, Maybeck used exterior details such as earthy cedar-shingle siding and painted elements that include ochre eaves, red rafters, and dark green window trim. The modern interiors function to bring in the surrounding nature. An abundance of oversized plate-glass windows and nine-foot-tall glazed French doors create a sense of intimacy with the gracefully tangled oaks and 100-year-old gardens. Were it not for the application of an unstained redwood trim on the interiors, the owner would be living in a glass tree house.

The light-filled, wide-open house proves ideal for showing off the contemporary and modern art collections of its owner, the art dealer Foster Goldstrom. Since purchasing the house 33 years ago, Goldstrom has become an enthusiastic connoisseur of all things Maybeck. He is passionate about learning the colorful history of the house and has been involved in researching it with members from each of the six families who have previously occupied it. Channeling Maybeck's sense of joy and wonderment of life, Goldstrom honors the Maybeckian tradition of frequently offering his home as a gathering place for friends old and new.

1981: Remodel of bathroom #1

1992: Remodel of bathroom #2

2000: Elevator removed

2003: Remodel of kitchen

Residence of Foster Goldstrom

Carolands

Hillsborough, 1916
Ernest Sanson, architect;
Achille Duchêne, architectural designer;
Willis Polk, managing architect

arolands is one of America's great country houses. It stands pristinely restored to its original magnificence, and though it was once set amid 554 hilltop acres, the 5.6 acres immediately surrounding the mansion today are beautifully and appropriately landscaped in the tradition of eighteenth-century French gardens. When the classically stylized French château was competed in 1916, its 98 rooms and 65,000 square feet of living space made it the largest personal residence west of the Mississippi. This was to be the new home for socialite couple Harriet Pullman and her husband, Francis J. Carolan, who had been married in 1892 and had taken their place among San Francisco's elite soon thereafter. Harriet was heiress to the Pullman luxury railroad car fortune, and she intended to impress her wealthy friends with the most splendid estate possible.

She was led by her sophisticated taste to hire preeminent École des Beaux Arts–trained French architect Ernest Sanson to design a mansion in the pure form of an eighteenth-century château. French landscape architect Achille Duchêne, who was well known in the social circles of the wealthy and had worked on many grand country houses in America and Europe, conceived an ambitious plan for the prominent site. Meanwhile, San Francisco architect Willis Polk would manage the construction. The team of prestigious architects would surely impress her society friends, and she would get her extravagant French château.

But this was not to be. Since its inception, the Beaux-Arts masterpiece has had a tumultuous history, twice being in danger of demolition. During the four years it took to

construct Carolands, the majority of Harriet's inheritance was tied up in investments tightly controlled by her mother, slowing and even halting Harriet's elaborate plans. By 1916, when her mother finally gave Harriet $1 million in Pullman stock with which to finish Carolands, Harriet had become disillusioned with both her marriage and the building of the house, making frequent visits instead to New York. Harriet sold Carolands in the mid-1940s and, thereafter, the house had several owners and the estate's land was subdivided. In 1950, when it was slated for demolition, the Countess Alessandro Dandini saved the mansion, but she was financially unable to restore it properly before her death in 1973.

When the current owners purchased Carolands in 1998, its condition had become ruinous. This visionary couple, however, not only saved the grand house, but managed to preserve the iconic treasure for generations to come, completing a five-year, multimillion-dollar restoration in 2003, noted for its authenticity and thoroughness. Overseeing the mammoth project, the wife also worked closely with renowned American interior designer Mario Buatta to create a splendid interior décor worthy of the architecture. The highly accomplished British landscape architect Martin Lane Fox redesigned the grounds by creating evocative gardens in the French eighteenth-century formal style. Now a private residence, the château has been thoroughly revived and brought back to its original glory. It is the owners' generous gift to California's architectural history and the world's architectural heritage.

OPPOSITE AND RIGHT

A monolithic atrium rises four stories at the center of the mansion. A huge metal and glass monitor skylight fills the core of the house with light. Gallery halls rimmed with colonnades of substantial Doric and Ionic columns and an ornate painted cast iron and gold-gilt balustrade, custom designed by architect Ernest Sanson, define the breathtaking space.

FOLLOWING PAGES

The expansive entrance hall that runs eighty feet along the width of the house serves as a spacious reception area. The magnificent grand staircase rises elegantly from the interior foyer to intermediate landings, then to the first floor galleries, off of which are located the (public) rooms of state.

OPPOSITE *During the five-year, multimillion-dollar restoration, the owner worked carefully with internationally renowned interior designer Mario Buatta. Their realized vision for the dramatically proportioned studio with its twenty-one-foot-high ceiling transformed it into a luxurious and comfortable formal salon. Complementing the décor are the grisaille paintings and Sanson-designed boiseries.*

RIGHT *The glamorous Chinese room is decorated with antique lacquered Coromandel panels. During the restoration, artist Robert Jackson's trompe l'oeil work replaced some of the wire mesh panels that had fronted cabinets for displaying Chinese objets d'art. The original carpet was found and installed.*

FOLLOWING PAGES *Gilded and faux-marbled walls, tall windows treated with luxurious cotton taffeta draperies, an impressive table that seats twenty-four, and sparkling crystal chandeliers create an atmosphere of opulence in the forty-foot-long formal dining room.*

PRECEDING PAGES *The library
is a spacious and light-filled room
that is made warm with earth-toned
upholstery and floor-to-ceiling
French-polished oak paneling carved
with design elements from the
French Rococo and Neoclassical
periods. An upper balcony with
carved Louis XV–style bookcases
is accessed by a private staircase and
overlooks the vast room. Three sets
of seventeen-foot-tall French doors
fill the south wall.*

ABOVE AND OPPOSITE
*The central circular element that
dominates the west facade was created
to accommodate the installation of the
26-foot-diameter circular room, one
of the two exquisite 1780 Bordeaux
salons that were purchased by
Harriet Pullman in 1912 in Paris.
The house was designed from 1913
to 1914 to accommodate the historic
boiseries in their eighteenth-century
arrangement. A copy of the original
floor is an inlaid design of rare
hardwoods.*

OPPOSITE *The main kitchen on the ground floor is designed with a dramatic flair. It has its original glazed cabinetry, a ceiling of milk-glass tiles, its original coal-fired range turned into the center island, and a visually striking original black stove and hood.*

RIGHT *Sanson's design for the pantry set it in an accommodating position between the dining room and the staff hallway, with a staircase, elevator, and dumbwaiter for access to any of the house's levels. Walls along the second-story balcony have built-in shelves and cupboards. The room features an unusual double-width German silver sink.*

FOLLOWING PAGES *Landscaping based on eighteenth-century French garden design includes that of the entrance court. Martin Lane Fox, former vice chairman of the Royal Horticultural Society, redesigned all of the gardens at Carolands.*

2003: Restoration and renovation

2003: Renovation of east terrace, new underground garage by Page & Turnbull, Inc., architects

California Historical Landmark

Listed on the National Register of Historic Places

Filoli House and Garden

Woodside, 1917
Willis J. Polk, architect

illiam Bowers Bourn, II, was one of San Francisco's wealthiest businessmen and a brilliant
entrepreneur who took over the operation of the Empire Mine in 1878 and struck a large
vein of ore five years later, making the gold mine the richest in the history of California.

In 1915, he commissioned San Francisco architect Willis J. Polk to design a substantial
family house in Woodside, south of San Francisco, an area on the Peninsula favored by the
wealthy after their exodus from the city following the 1906 earthquake. Polk had previously
designed two houses for the Bourn family: their summer residence, Empire Cottage, in Grass
Valley near the gold mine, and a finely articulated brick-and-stone townhouse in Pacific
Heights. Between 1916 and 1920, Bourn hired San Francisco architect Arthur Brown, Jr., to
design a carriage house, a garden pavilion, and a garden hardscape with auxiliary buildings.

Bourn chose to call the grand country estate Filoli, an acronym for his life philosophy
created with the first two letters in its key words: "Fight for a just cause; love your fellow
man; live a good life." The magnificent brick mansion combines elements of the Georgian
Revival with those of the Neoclassical and various Mediterranean styles. Its 654 acres of
pristine landscape, with views of Crystal Springs Lake and the wooded eastern slope of
the coastal range south of San Francisco, is unsurpassed. Land adjoining that of the Spring
Valley Water Company (supplier of water to San Francisco) was purchased by Bourn in
1908. His land was protected from further development by law.

Artist and landscape designer Bruce Porter collaborated with Bourn on the landscaping of 16 acres of formal gardens that were laid out from 1917 to 1922. Bella Worn, who had worked for both the Bourns and the following owners, the Roths, chose the planting materials following the style of gardens created for the smaller seventeenth-century manor houses in England and Scotland.

The spectacular gardens of Filoli first became world renowned under the stewardship of William P. and Lurline Matson Roth, who purchased the estate in 1937. Filoli became a social center for the family of five. In 1941, daughter Berenice was married in the only wedding to have taken place at Filoli.

By 1927, William P. Roth had risen to the title of president in his father-in-law William Matson's shipping empire, the Matson Navigational Company. He added to both the company's and his personal fortune by expanding a fleet of luxury cruise ships and building upscale hotels in Hawaii during the 1930s. Roth died in 1963, and in 1975 his widow, Lurline, donated the house and gardens to the National Trust for Historic Preservation. Both of the Roths enjoyed the gardens immensely, but it was Lurline, always a keen gardener, who had built the international reputation of Filoli by hosting horticultural, botanical, and gardening societies. This tradition continues today at Filoli, now a historic house and garden. It is maintained by a dedicated professional staff and a team of 1,100 enthusiastic volunteers and is open to the public from February to November.

PRECEDING PAGES *A portrait of Mrs. Agnes Moody Bourn, wife of William Bowers Bourn II, painted by Sir William Orpen in 1916, hangs in a place of honor in the American black walnut–paneled library.*

RIGHT *A portion of the drawing room is devoted to an intimate seating area with an ornately decorative painted eighteenth-century Italian harpsichord.*

1920: Carriage house, garden pavilion, garden hardscape, auxiliary buildings by Arthur Brown, Jr., architect

1946: Swimming pool

1996: Visitor and Education Center

California Historical Landmark

Owned by the National Trust for Historic Preservation; administered by Filoli Center in a co-stewardship agreement

LEFT   *The kitchen at Filoli has remained delightfully unchanged since the Roth era and is fully functional.*

RIGHT   *A spectacular design of the second-floor landing of the main staircase uses tall engaged Corinthian columns and pillars and a high arched window to give the space grandeur.*

FOLLOWING PAGES   *The garden pavilion serves as a conservatory where the mingled heady scents of various flowers may be enjoyed.*

LEFT *The Petit Trianon at Versailles was the inspiration for architect Arthur Brown, Jr.'s, design of the brick pavilion in 1920.*

BELOW LEFT *The carriage house, designed by Arthur Brown, Jr., and now used as the gift and garden shop, is topped with a distinctive cupola.*

RIGHT *One of Filoli's themed garden "rooms" is the Sundial Garden Area. Here, a brick pathway, with an antique sundial as a focal point, divides parterres of English Boxwood and ornamental flowers. Grecian Bay Laurel are sheared into cylindrical columns.*

FOLLOWING PAGES *The centerpiece of the peaceful symmetrical design of the Sunken Garden is a reflecting pool surrounded by beautifully manicured lawns, colorful pansies in containers, tall Foxglove (Digitalis), and Baby Blue-Eyes (Nemophila) in the low beds.*

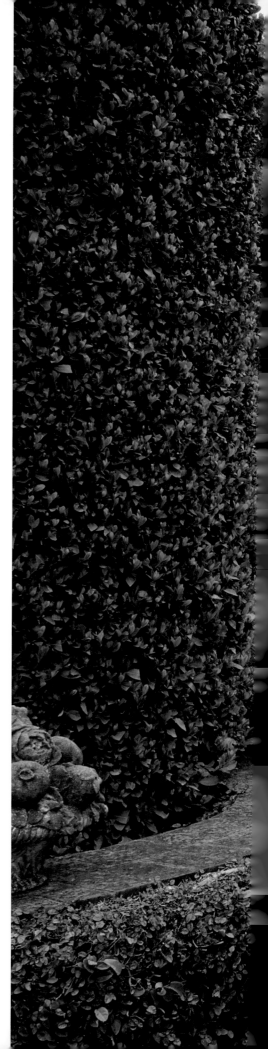

Lou Henry Hoover House

Stanford, 1920
Arthur B. Clark, architect;
Lou Henry Hoover, architectural designer

PRECEDING PAGES *Lou Henry Hoover, wife of U.S. President Herbert Hoover, designed the eighteen-thousand-square-foot, multilevel family residence at Stanford with architect and art professor Arthur B. Clark. The house creatively combines architectural design elements from the Pueblo, Mission Revival, Modernist, and International styles as well as vernacular elements from adobes of the American Southwest and North Africa.*

LEFT *The interior features elements that reflect the traditional style of the Hoovers' former London residence, Red House. Mrs. Hoover's love of leaded-glass windows prevailed in the oak-paneled dining room.*

OPPOSITE *Carved oak accents in the inviting foyer include a Neoclassical surround of the arched doorway, hefty ceiling beams, and stair balustrades designed with a Gothic motif.*

*D*own a private lane that runs along San Juan Hill in the faculty housing area of Stanford University, surrounded by a mature landscape of towering trees and well-manicured formal gardens, is the house that has served as the home of each of the presidents of Stanford University since 1945. Lou Henry Hoover, wife of U.S. President Herbert Hoover, designed the house, which was built from 1919 to 1920, to be their permanent family home.

The Hoovers had met as undergraduates in the geology department at Stanford, which held a special place in their hearts and to which they had always hoped to return. Because of Hoover's career in the mining industry prior to his becoming president, the couple moved frequently. In 1899, Hoover's work first took the couple to China, and later England, Australia, Burma, and the East Coast of the U.S. In their extensive travels, they also became familiar with the cultures of Japan, New Zealand, Samoa, Ceylon, Egypt, South Africa, various countries in Europe, and the American Southwest. In 1918, as the Hoovers were commuting between California and the East Coast, they took the opportunity to build this longed-for permanent residence on five acres. The house would be the Hoovers' "real" home, as Lou referred to it. Although they did not live there year-round, it was always their residence for summers and special events. After Lou's passing in 1944, Herbert Hoover bequeathed the house to Stanford University.

PRECEDING PAGES *"A very soft shade of natural oak," is how Lou Henry described the paneling and carved wood accents she designed for the living room. Its coved ceiling was lit indirectly with bulbs in the cove. The ceiling's beam design is reminiscent of a luxurious Pullman railway car.*

RIGHT *A fireplace with a distinctive surround and chimney breast dominates one section of the living room. Shallow steps at one end of the living room lead to a raised, narrow alcove room, designed with an old-world feeling featuring a wall of leaded-glass doors and windows. The room was used to display gifts from the Belgian people for Hoover's food-relief assistance during the First World War.*

Of particular interest to Lou was the architecture of the world's "primitive" cultures. Her love of early architectural forms created a personal preference for practical and utilitarian houses in a simple, unadorned style. And though the Hoovers had become quite wealthy, Lou eschewed ostentation of any kind, including imposing, formal, ornamented architecture.

The design of the 18,000-square-foot, three-level house mitigates its size. The lower level is built into the hillside and is not visible on the entrance facade at the main level. Flat roofs cleverly serve as terraces, accessed by glazed French doors in each room that create an easy flow between indoor and outdoor environments, emphasizing Lou's strong belief in the importance and health benefits of living with fresh air. Arthur Bridgman Clark, Stanford's professor of art and design, is the architect of record, but he rightly credits Lou Henry Hoover as the principal designer.

RIGHT *The design of the three-level house, with its massing of piled cubes and unornamented planar stucco surfaces, mitigates its size. Flat roofs cleverly serve as terraces, accessed by glazed French doors in each room.*

The design was specifically not a historic or period-revival piece. And though it has been described stylistically as Pueblo, Mission Revival, Modernist, or International, among others, the simple adobe forms reminiscent of North Africa and the American Southwest seem to have inspired or at least been referenced in the house's massing of piled cubes and unornamented planar stucco surfaces. Guided by her affinity for simple building forms that she had admired in her travels and studies, Lou created a highly functional, visually pleasing, unpretentious (albeit large) home that served her family well. It continues to serve the president of Stanford University and his family today as a comfortable home as well as a center for entertaining thousands of university visitors each year.

National Historic Landmark

California Historical Landmark

Listed on the National Register of Historic Places

Owned by Stanford University

George Fox Steedman Estate, Casa del Herrero

Montecito, 1925

George Washington Smith, architect

PRECEDING PAGES *Santa Barbara architect George Washington Smith designed The George Fox Steedman estate, Casa del Herrero, in 1925. It is one of the finest examples of Spanish Revival and Spanish Colonial Revival architecture in America and, accordingly, has been deemed a National Historic Landmark.*

LEFT *The second-floor hallway leads from the private bedrooms to the servants' quarters and back stairwell. A dado of colorful antique Spanish tiles and a high ceiling masterfully reinforce the linear quality of the space. The spectacular seventeenth-century Mudéjar doors and frame purchased by Steedman in Seville are from Écija.*

OPPOSITE *The entrance hall dazzles with its elaborate fifteenth-century Spanish* artesonado *(decorated ceiling) consisting of forty-eight wood panels painted with small pictures and embellished with other paintings and carvings, a fifteenth-century Flemish tapestry, one of Steedman's costliest purchases, and antique Spanish furnishings that include a late sixteenth-century misericord (carved ecclesiastical seating). Tile insets in the flooring are sixteenth-century Spanish.*

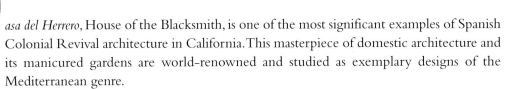

asa del Herrero, House of the Blacksmith, is one of the most significant examples of Spanish Colonial Revival architecture in California. This masterpiece of domestic architecture and its manicured gardens are world-renowned and studied as exemplary designs of the Mediterranean genre.

The charm and beauty of the seven-acre estate lie in the combination of its essential parts. The residence is uniquely ornamented with antique architectural fragments and examples of the finely crafted metalwork by its original owner. Among its furnishings are treasures acquired throughout Spain, including many sixteenth-century ecclesiastical pieces. The property's landscaping features garden rooms defined by their usage, namely the cutting and kitchen gardens, or by their architectural elements, such as the antique marble columns and arched openings that semi-enclose the east patio.

The house was a creative and meticulous collaboration between Santa Barbara architect George Washington Smith, the preeminent designer in the Spanish Revival and Spanish Colonial Revival styles, and its artistic, intelligent owner, George Fox Steedman, a successful retired industrialist from St. Louis who enthusiastically and obsessively oversaw every detail of the design and construction.

Like *La Questa Encantada*, William Randolph Hearst's San Simeon retreat, the interiors here are a repository for a collection of priceless Spanish antiques—furniture, decorative

PRECEDING PAGES *The main living room is furnished with Spanish antiques and art that were carefully chosen by Steedman or his agents in Spain, Arthur Byne and Mildred Stapley, who also bought for such other clients as William Randolph Hearst.*

LEFT *A small, octagonal Gothic-style book tower designed by architect Lutah Maria Riggs was added in 1933. Riggs, who had worked closely with George Washington Smith in his firm, incorporated such evocative details as a Mexican silver chandelier and frieze panels painted and gilded by Santa Barbara artist Channing Peake.*

RIGHT AND FOLLOWING PAGES *The dining room features a gleaming floor inset with small sixteenth-century Spanish tiles, stair risers decorated with colorful custom-designed tiles fabricated in Tunisia by* Les Fils de Chemla, *antique carved wooden doors, and antique Spanish ecclesiastical processional standards repurposed as lamps. The bronze lion finial was bought by Steedman in Spain and used as a model from which he reproduced matching finials on the loggia.*

objects, artwork, and architectural fragments. The well-connected American antiquarians Arthur Byne and his wife, Mildred Stapley, who were living in Spain, guided Steedman and his friend Louis La Beaume, a St. Louis architect, on a seven-week tour of the country in 1923, counseling them on purchases of antique furnishings and decorative art pieces; the couple continued to make purchases on behalf of Steedman after he returned to the United States. Byne and Stapley also arranged for the procurement of thousands of decorative glazed tiles from Les Files de Chemla in Tunisia.

The general landscape scheme that placed formal gardens near the house and less formally planted sections farther away was the plan of Ralph T. Stevens. In 1925, however, Steedman decided to revise the garden design, and he hired Lockwood de Forest, Jr., a noted Santa Barbara landscape architect, and Francis T. Underhill, an acquaintance of Steedman's who had a talent for architectural and landscape design. De Forest and Underhill changed the plan to give it more impact and included features such as pergolas and benches at the bottom of the lawn and a tiled fountain in the entry auto court.

George Steedman's daughter, Medora Bass, inherited the estate, and after the death of her husband, she wished to see the casa preserved intact for public benefit. With the guidance and financial support of Medora's son, George Bass, the Casa del Herrero Foundation was formed to fulfill this imperative. As owner and guardian, the foundation regularly opens the house and gardens to the public as well as the scholars of California's architectural and horticultural history.

LEFT *The focal point of the master bedroom is the magnificent inglenook fireplace, with a wall design of interlocking patterns of sixteenth-century tiles, a line of antique Alcora figure tiles, and modern* Les Fils de Chemla *tile borders.*

BELOW LEFT *The house contains over 17,000 decorative tiles. In the downstairs beauty parlor (powder room), colorful glazed tile was used profusely and to great effect. The splendid display of tile work includes some nine patterns of Chemla tile and Alcora and Catalan figure tiles. A brass oil lamp that has been refitted into an electric light illuminates the sparkling tiled surfaces.*

OPPOSITE *A tiled window bench and intimate fireplace create charm in Mrs. Steedman's upstairs bedroom.*

LEFT *A major axis of the house runs east to west, with an enfilade that stretches the width of the house. The tiled exedra fountain seen in the distance through the living room doorway is sited as the focal point at the terminus of the east–west axis.*

OPPOSITE *Smith incorporated many antique architectural fragments into the exterior design. A carved stone Byzantine door frame decorates an entry doorway to the western garden.*

RIGHT *The Spanish Garden's design was inspired by the arcaded walls at the Generalife, a summer palace near the Alhambra, a fourteenth-century fortress in Granada, Spain. Hand-wrought iron curtain rods along the walls once held draperies that could be closed to make the space even more intimate.*

FOLLOWING PAGES

PAGES 222–223 *The pepper tree fountain designed with antique Spanish tiles defines the walled garden at the southern end of the estate. Landscape architect Lockwood de Forest, Jr., and socialite and architectural designer Francis T. Underhill worked on modifications of the garden design with input from Steedman after 1925.*

PAGES 224–225 *The south facade of the house is a masterful study of asymmetry, where antique carved stone elements distinguish windows and arches. Inspired by the Moorish gardens in Spain, an underground and aboveground tiled runnel carries water from fountain to fountain along the north–south axis of the backyard.*

1929: Butler's cottage, well house by Edwards, Plunkett & Howell, architects

1933: Book tower, remodel of garages by Lutah Maria Riggs, architect; New workshop; Floyd Brewster, architect

National Historic Landmark

Listed on the National Register of Historic Places

Owned by The Casa del Herrero Foundation

Crocker-Fagan Mansion

Pebble Beach, 1928
George Washington Smith, architect

ne of architect George Washington Smith's most unusual designs and extravagant commissions was the Pebble Beach retreat for irrepressible bon vivant Charles Templeton Crocker, heir to the Crocker railroad fortune, and his wife, Helele Irwin, an heiress whose millions came from her father's Hawaiian sugar plantations. The couple's main residence, Uplands, was a 35,000-square-foot mansion designed by San Francisco architect Willis Polk situated on 500 acres in the exclusive enclave of Hillsborough.

Pebble Beach, the beautiful forested and seaside area comprising the western half of the Monterey Peninsula that is known today for its luxurious spas and internationally renowned golf courses, first became a resort site in 1880 with the opening of the elegant Hotel Del Monte and a connecting express railroad from the Pacific Improvement Company, owned by California's Big Four. The company created the scenic 17-Mile Drive a year later and in 1907 offered coastal building lots. The Templeton Crocker House was built on a rocky promontory along this wind-swept part of the Pacific Coast, the site dense with spectacular aged Monterey cypress trees.

Smith attended to every detail during the lengthy design process and oversaw construction of the house from his Santa Barbara office 250 miles south. Beginning in 1923, the conceptual drawings reveal two other major designs: a Moorish–Spanish Revival–style house massed with flat-roofed cubes and a half-timbered Tudor Revival–style house that

PRECEDING PAGES *All of the architectural details of the house were designed specifically for it by Smith, save the sixteenth-century carved stone fireplace mantel from an Italian church. The main entrance is a cloister with a garden surrounded by 22 pairs of carved columns in 32 differing shades of Italian marble. Capitals for each pair of columns were elaborately carved with different designs of Byzantine character.*

RIGHT *For the entry floor's inlaid marble mosaic, Smith's associate, architect Lutah Maria Riggs, designed a circular pattern surrounded by signs of the zodiac and framed by compass points and place names in Greek.*

contained a corner tower and turrets. But the final design choice, made in May 1926, was that of a Byzantine-style mansion resembling a stone monastery.

Enriching the design was an abundance of exterior and interior details, many drawn to full scale. Each element of the house would be new. No antique fragments were to be used. Plans also revealed interiors filled with specialized decorations. Most spectacular are the use of exotic Italian marbles, the gold Venetian-glass tile mosaics, and a wall treatment for the dining room that featured a Byzantine-style mural with inlaid semiprecious stones.

The Crockers had married in 1911 and were divorced in 1928. Thereafter, Templeton Crocker was not a part of the Pebble Beach project, but Helene continued its construction. In 1929, she married a Hillsborough neighbor, successful businessman Paul Fagan. In the mid-1940s, they retired to Hawaii, where Paul started Hana Ranch and what later became the Hotel Hana-Maui, both on Maui. Fagan died in 1960.

Templeton Crocker kept Uplands but visited only intermittently. He pursued a variety of interests and became a noted contributor to the arts and sciences. He produced an opera he had written in 1917 to great acclaim in Europe and several San Francisco venues. He traveled the globe during the 1930s in his

OPPOSITE AND RIGHT
The dining room's wainscoting of carved Doria stone anchors the Byzantine mosaics, originally inset with precious stones, that cover the walls and vaulted ceiling. During an extensive restoration, the present owner had Italian artisans restore the paintings.

118-foot yacht, *Zaca*, collecting data for such institutions as the California Academy of Sciences and the American Museum of Natural History. This included an unprecedented collection of invaluable data, thousands of photographs, and many reels of 16mm film. And in 1940, he donated his impressive book collection to the California Historical Society, which he had helped found. These cultural contributions that resulted from Crocker's innately adventurous spirit and curious mind are a worthy legacy.

After the mansion's purchase in a dilapidated condition, the current owner's careful restoration, undertaken from 1999 to 2005, returned the mansion to Smith's original standards.

ABOVE AND OPPOSITE *In the master bathroom, one of six large bathrooms in the house, cut and layered abalone shells cover the vaulted ceiling, and gold Venetian-glass tile mosaics cover the floor and rim of the carved black marble tub. Bronze grilles are designed with a Byzantine pattern as are the capitals of the black marble columns throughout the room.*

LEFT *A grand circular stone staircase with Crazan stone walls ascends to the second floor in the tower. Leaded-glass clerestory windows trimmed in Crazan stone and a colorful Byzantine-themed painted domed ceiling make the space spectacular.*

OPPOSITE *At the entrance to the house from the motor court, the overwhelming grandeur of the monastic-like structure is tempered by the intimacy of a small garden within the series of carved Italian marble columns. The column capitals' intricately carved Byzantine designs add delicacy and interest to the space.*

FOLLOWING PAGES *The two-foot-thick stone walls are durable and sturdy, withstanding the wind and salt water that assault the westerly facade. From the terrace, a breathtaking 180-degree view of the California coastline is enlivened by tumultuous Pacific Ocean waves crashing on the boulders a hundred feet below.*

2005: Remodel; restoration of dining room murals

C.K.G. **Billings–Emmons Estate**

Montecito, 1929

Carleton Monroe Winslow, architect

PRECEDING PAGES
*Robert and Christine
Emmons have meticulously
restored the famous Spanish
Colonial Revival mansion
built for New York tycoon
and horse breeder C. K. G.
Billings to its evocative
1929 design.*

LEFT AND OPPOSITE
*The Emmonses have placed
large sculptural pieces from
their impressive collection
within the landscaped
grounds and within the
iconic arcade that defines
the front of the house.*

fter their 1992 purchase of the abandoned C. K. G. Billings Estate in Montecito, Robert and Christine Emmons researched details of its fascinating history and were determined to restore and renovate the iconic landmark correctly. Their choice for what turned out to be an extensive three-year project was well-known Santa Barbara architectural designer Michael De Rose, who they felt could best recapture the essence that had made this one of the most famous of the magnificent California estates built during the 1920s.

The Emmonses' intention was to return the Spanish Colonial Revival–style house to its 1929 design. The multilevel residence with commanding views of the Santa Barbara Channel and Pacific coastline, was designed by Carlton Monroe Winslow as the centerpiece of the 188-acre estate of New York tycoon C. K. G. Billings. It replaced the villa that Francis T. Underhill had designed in 1919, which had been irreparably damaged in the 1925 earthquake.

Cornelius Kingsley Garrison Billings was one of the wealthiest men in America, with a fortune in 1913 estimated at $30 million. Much of his wealth came from Union Carbide and Carbon, which he cofounded and for which he served as chairman of the board from 1929 until his death in 1937.

*Architectural details in the
interior such as fully arched
door and window openings,
intricate hand-wrought
ironwork that reveals the lush
gardens outside, and polished
inlaid wood and patterned
stone flooring create a refined
atmosphere for the Emmonses'
world-class art collection.
Contemporary life-size
Florentine bronzes set a tone
of grandeur for the entrance
hall gallery.*

LEFT *Rare seventeenth-century English oak panels in the dining room contain sections with linenfold designs as well as other ornately carved motifs.*

OPPOSITE *The magnificent carved oak staircase, a work of art that features ornately carved balustrades and newel post, leads to the private quarters on the upper level.*

FOLLOWING PAGES *Christine Emmons researched and selected the Barbizon School paintings for the dining room, which are in keeping with C. K.G. Billings's original art collection. Incorporated into the current dining room are early seventeenth-century English carved oak–paneled walls that were previously installed in the villa designed by Francis T. Underhill that was built on the site for Billings in 1919. The panels were salvaged after the Santa Barbara earthquake of 1925 destroyed the villa.*

Billings led a flamboyant and extravagant life filled with an array of interests and pleasures. At one time, it was reported that Billings owned the finest collection of art in America. He was also an avid yachtsman whose most spectacular schooner was the 240-foot custom-made German vessel *Vandis*. But his first and greatest love was horses. He was a passionate horseman and horse breeder, owning Thoroughbreds that included two world-record-setting trotters and the Kentucky Derby winner of 1917. Enjoying his horses was one of the main reasons for his moving to California. Billings kept his prized champion Thoroughbreds and other horses, which he rode often, at his beautiful Asombrosso stables on his Montecito estate.

His vast real estate holdings included commercial investments in New York City and large horse-breeding farms on Long Island and near Richmond, Virginia. Tryon Hall, his estate and Louis XIV–style mansion on the Hudson River, was purchased in 1917 by John D. Rockefeller, Jr., who donated it to the City of New York for a park. It now includes the Cloisters, an annex of the Metropolitan Museum of Art.

Within two weeks of selling Tryon Hall, Billings moved to Santa Barbara and began to purchase land in Montecito, where he would live for the rest of his life. Billings became one of Santa Barbara's greatest philanthropists, along with the other civic-minded "hill barons," such as Frederick Forrest Peabody, of Arrow

LEFT *A portion of an extended terrace features an outdoor fireplace and vantage points from which to enjoy the gardens below and the sweeping view of the Pacific Ocean.*

OPPOSITE *From the reflecting pool to the northwest of the house with an Alhambra lion carved stone fountain, the arcade at the front of the house creates an intimate space for contemporary sculpture, such as those from the Florence Academy of Art, seen in the distance.*

FOLLOWING PAGES *The lush landscaping of the Billings–Emmons Estate includes vast lawns, mature palms, hedges that partition separate spaces for such areas as the pool and pool house, and a formal rose garden with boxwood parterres. The back terrace overlooks the gardens and lower lawn with Montecito and the Pacific Ocean beyond.*

shirt fame; George Owen Knapp, his neighbor and cofounder of the Union Carbide Company; and David Gray, whose father helped finance Henry Ford. Their collective generosity and foresight during the 1920s created many of the institutions and public spaces that make Santa Barbara what it is today.

Robert and Christine Emmons have followed Billings's lead, becoming avid collectors of eighteenth- and nineteenth-century European art. But their similarity to Billings doesn't end there. For years, the philanthropic pair have made major contributions to a variety of Santa Barbara nonprofits, giving generously of their time and resources. The Billings–Emmons Estate, now returned to its serene elegance, once again provides an appropriate setting for a lively and generous civic-minded couple who appreciate the beauty and culture of Santa Barbara.

1929: New residence (that incorporated portions of the 1919 structure designed by Francis T. Underhill) by Carleton Monroe Winslow, architect

1996: Restoration and renovation by Michael De Rose, architectural designer

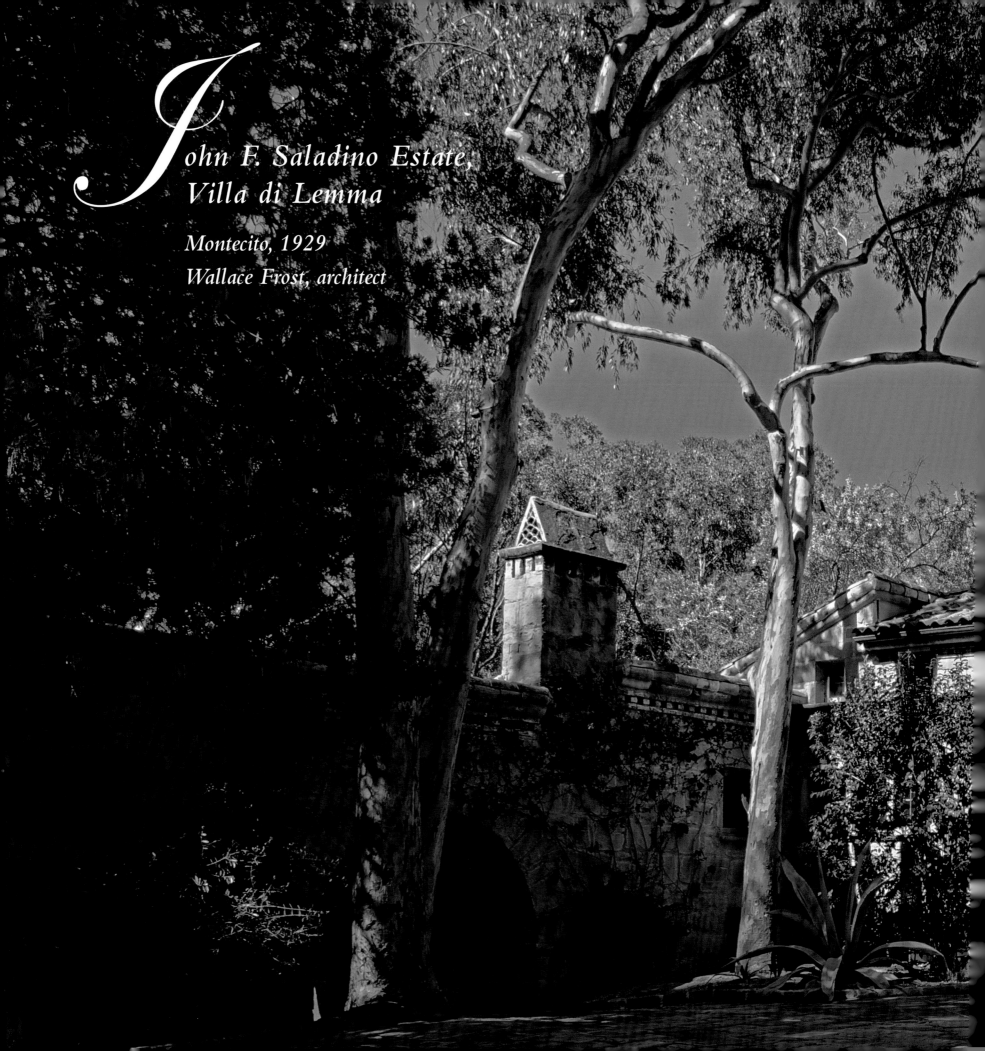

*J*ohn F. Saladino Estate,
Villa di Lemma

Montecito, 1929
Wallace Frost, architect

PRECEDING PAGES *Internationally renowned architectural and interior designer John F. Saladino's four-year restoration and remodel of the ruins of a historic stone villa and re–design of the overgrown 12-and-a-half-acre estate in Montecito yielded a magnificent world-class residence.*

LEFT *Lush plantings complement the Juliet balcony, one of the many architectural details that Saladino has perfected to enhance the historic essence of the villa.*

OPPOSITE *The enclosed entrance gallery with rustic stone walls, heavy wood beams, and Saladino's iconic luxurious drapery treatment at the opening to the motor court, serves as a sheltering, peaceful space before entering the villa.*

ohn Saladino is a true artist, an old soul with a young heart, and a romantic. While his graduate work at Yale University taught him to adopt a minimalist approach toward architectural design and his early profession as a painter reinforced his innate sense of color, it was while working in Rome for two years that his mind and soul were opened to the unlimited possibilities of a sensual world. During his sojourn in the city, he became captivated by Roman antiquity. While in Rome, he acknowledged an affinity for theatrical scale and the importance of an emotional response, both of which inform his work today. He imbues his rooms, inside and out, with romance and drama, a quality that resulted from his immersion in the ancient city.

Saladino is also an acute businessman with a large firm and the manufacturer of a line of furniture that includes 80 pieces of his own design. At 73, he is one of the most successful and enduring internationally renowned designers in the world. While his goal is always to create a place of serenity and beauty, he understands, too, that practical considerations are necessary. His intellectual prowess allows him to vividly explain what he sees and feels. And he delivers.

Balance, he insists, is the key. Supposed opposites when juxtaposed give a powerful, dramatic effect. Classical and contemporary, smooth and textured, grand and intimate, large

ABOVE *In the drawing room, Saladino's mastery of light, color, and scale is brilliantly evident. Sumptuous fabrics on sofas of his own design, seventeenth-century chairs, and a tapestry-clothed ottoman imbue this large space with sensuality and comfort.*

OPPOSITE *A diminutive fireplace in the entrance hall adds whimsy and warmth to the intimate space. A Renaissance candle sconce is positioned above one of a pair of seventeenth-century Italian sgabelli chairs. Walnut double doors and an antique Kula prayer rug lead into the drawing room.*

RIGHT *The powder room, which Saladino has christened the "gossip," epitomizes the masterful balance between beauty and practicality that is the designer's hallmark. A Roman sink receives water from a seventeenth-century Turkish faucet, while an eighteenth-century Austrian blue glass courting mirror hangs at eye level above.*

RIGHT *In the cozy and elegant dining room, Saladino and his guests, seated in comfortable Villa chairs of their host's design, dine by candlelight from a five-foot-diameter country French chandelier. The original wood paneling has been stripped of old paint and washed with a light gray stain.*

FOLLOWING PAGES *The wide arch originally framed an open porch. Now fully glazed, it frames the breakfast room wall facing the Oriental carpet terrace, ingeniously creates a grand entrance to the "stage" of the outdoor gardens, and also allows sunlight into the kitchen.*

and small, dark and light, European traditions and twenty-first-century American concepts—all blend seamlessly in Saladino's singular designs.

His vacation home in Santa Barbara is a historic stone farmhouse or, what some might call an intimate villa in Montecito's hills, and it became a palette for his numerous talents. A brief first sighting of the run-down house and grounds in 1985 sparked his imagination and, years later, in 2001, he bought the 12-and-a-half-acre estate with a clear vision of its eventual glory. Although built of locally quarried sandstone by East Coast architect Wallace Frost in 1929, the house and landscaping had become ruins. Saladino embarked upon a complex four-year restoration and remodel of the entire house, accommodating it for twenty-first-century technology and comfort while returning it aesthetically to the essence of its historical roots.

His design for the estate's wooded acreage included creating an appropriately elegant yet casual atmosphere that blended with the surrounding California landscape. Gardens painted in blue-gray-silver tones, emerald lawn "carpets" edged in blocks of

OPPOSITE *In his bathroom, Saladino raised the ceiling substantially, evidenced by the placement of the original beam holes, and created a large coffered skylight. The corner fireplace is useful and picturesque, as is the small leaded-glass window.*

ABOVE *In the guest bedroom, a muted palette creates serenity and peace. French doors open to a private hedged garden.*

ABOVE *An ancient Roman column marking the southwest corner of the pool terrace bids the onlooker to contemplate centuries past and the vast Pacific Ocean beyond.*

RIGHT *Saladino has landscaped the area immediately surrounding the villa with manicured and themed gardens, the blue, gray, and silver plantings of which reflect the muted and restful palette of the villa's interiors.*

RIGHT *Saladino's mastery of landscape architecture is evident in the textural layering and juxtaposition of plantings that surround the villa. Intimate spaces, such as this secluded garden and sitting area off of a guest suite, epitomize the villa's romance.*

FOLLOWING PAGES *At the back of the house, two lengthy stone steps lead from the lawn-covered Oriental carpet terrace to an outdoor graveled family dining area shaded by a stand of venerable olive trees.*

honey-toned sandstone, an atrium courtyard accented with ancient marble sculpture, and a stunning allée of aged olive trees highlight the landscape and harmonize with the same blue-gray palette Saladino has chosen for the interior.

Villa di Lemma, his tongue-in-cheek name for the estate, is his dream, his paradise. He is surrounded by beauty and immersed in a vision of the ancient world that inspires him. Perhaps the corner of the estate that epitomizes its essence best is the lower grass terrace surrounding the swimming pool, where a Roman column leads the eye to a peaceful view of the Montecito hills and distant Pacific Ocean. Saladino, the artist, has created a world of peace and serenity.

2004: Remodel by John Saladino, architectural designer; Stephen Barlow, architect; and Naoko Kondo, Sr., designer, Saladino Group, Inc.

Hearst Castle, San Simeon, La Cuesta Encantada

San Simeon, 1919–37, 1945–47
Julia Morgan, architect

an Simeon, better known as Hearst Castle, is awe-inspiring and wondrous. The hilltop village-like complex with four main buildings designed in the Spanish Colonial Revival and Mediterranean styles overlooks the Pacific Ocean and miles of California coast. It was built as a residence for William Randolph Hearst, where his extensive collections of valuable European antique furnishings, large architectural pieces, and art could be showcased in lavish interiors. The "ranch," as he called it, would also be the place where he entertained his many famous guests. It served, too, as his command post for the Hearst media empire.

Set in a 127-acre landscape of manicured gardens and mature plantings, its three villas, each containing multiple guest suites, faced Casa Grande, the main house. Among other structures that Hearst commissioned for the enjoyment of his guests were two classically designed swimming pools, a tennis court, and a mile-long arbor under which guests could ride on horseback. San Simeon was truly an enchanted world unto itself.

When he was a boy, Hearst loved going to Camp Hill, his family's retreat of about 40,000 acres made up of former ranchlands that his father had begun acquiring in 1865. Its gently rolling hills and miles of beachfront were located midway between San Francisco and Los Angeles. In 1919, Hearst inherited the ranch from his father, and he would eventually expand it to 250,000 acres. He began planning for a residence that would afford phenomenal views of the California coastline, vistas that would become preeminent in the

ABOVE *The Gothic Study's colorful arches were painted in 1934 and inspired by medieval scenes decorating a fourteenth-century Sicilian ceiling.*

RIGHT *The entire third floor of Casa Grande was Hearst's private quarters and aptly named the Gothic Suite. His sitting room features a Gothic mantel and a barrel-vaulted ceiling that combines antique arches with twentieth-century wood coffers.*

FOLLOWING PAGES *The ground-floor, 2,500-square-foot Assembly Room was a sumptuously decorated living room and the social center of Casa Grande. Among the antique treasures integrated into its design are Italian Renaissance choir stalls, sixteenth-century Flemish tapestries, and marble bas-relief medallions by the nineteenth-century Danish sculptor Bertel Thorvaldsen.*

design of the hilltop palace. In 1924, Hearst changed the name from *Las Estrellas* (The Stars) to *La Cuesta Encantada* (The Enchanted Hill).

By the time Hearst was 56 and ready to begin the construction on his California land, he was heir to a multimillion-dollar fortune and was swiftly becoming a news-media tycoon. This robust, multitasking business genius hired the diminutive Julia Morgan, an extraordinarily competent architect and engineer. Her combination of technical and design skills enabled the successful completion of the magnificent structures at San Simeon, a project that lasted nearly three decades. Equally important to the success of the project were the similarities of Morgan's and Hearst's personalities and styles: both were perfectionists with extremely creative minds. She and Hearst were focused and dedicated to building San Simeon, and their high energy levels allowed them to keep up with each other.

ABOVE *The magnificent Gothic Study is one of two large libraries in Casa Grande. It was also used by Hearst as a boardroom. Carved and inlaid bookcases hold 3,000 books as well as metalwork and sculpture from the Gothic and Renaissance eras.*

RIGHT *Tracery windows at the far end of the Gothic Study heighten the ecclesiastical feeling of the space and frame a sweeping view of the mountains to the east.*

PRECEDING PAGES *The Morning Room is lit by antique Spanish and Italian silver lamps that hang from a sixteenth-century painted Spanish ceiling. The gilded altarpiece from Aragon is five hundred years old and depicts scenes from the life of St. Martin.*

LEFT *Curving arches frame a gilded and painted ceiling on the outside loggia of Casa del Sol.*

RIGHT *The grand Refectory or dining hall is strongly medieval in character, its atmosphere enlivened by a French Gothic mantelpiece, Flemish tapestries, and fourteenth- to fifteenth-century Spanish choir stalls. Guests ate all of their meals in this room.*

FOLLOWING PAGES
PAGES 288–289 *The luminescent indoor Roman pool was designed to resemble an ancient Roman bath. This enormous room is entirely covered with one-square-inch Murano-glass tiles of deep blue and shimmering gold. Many of the room's tile mosaics depict fanciful marine scenes.*

PAGES 290–291 *The spectacular Neptune Pool was enlarged and rebuilt several times over a 14-year period. In this final version, Morgan created a Classical Roman temple using fragments of antique columns, bases, and capitals combined with reproductions of ancient pieces. It is flanked by modern marble colonnades.*

PRECEDING PAGES *From the upper plaza of Casa Grande, a pair of small curved staircases descends to the cottage named* Casa del Mar. *Opposite its entrance stands the marble group* The Three Graces, *created by the nineteenth-century sculptor by Boyer, after Antonio Canova.*

LEFT *Casa del Monte has ten rooms: four bedrooms, four bathrooms, an entry loggia, and a sitting room. At 2,500 square feet, it is the smallest structure on the hilltop.*

BELOW, FAR LEFT *Fine cast-stone detailing on* Casa Grande*'s north facade's loggia balustrade complements the bold and highly ornate carved teakwood cornice.*

BELOW, NEAR LEFT *One of the most beautiful architectural elements at Hearst Castle is the Moorish balcony on the west side of* Casa del Sol. *In the purdah screen, mushrabiya, or intricate puzzle designs of numerous turned wood pieces, many painted and gilded, appear as latticework.*

OPPOSITE *In the entry loggia of* Casa del Monte, *gold-leafed plaster ornament decorates the ceiling, windows, and doors. The room's upper walls feature a seventeenth-century Venetian frieze by the Baroque artist Francesco Maffei.*

RIGHT *The walls of the Doge's Suite Sitting Room on* Casa Grande's *mezzanine are lined in a striking blue silk that creates a vibrant space. The ceiling features a centuries-old Dutch painting surrounded by painted panels depicting the eight virtues. These two separate ceiling fragments were joined and augmented by modern carved details to match the room's dimensions.*

While working for Hearst, Morgan commuted by train between her San Francisco office and San Simeon almost every weekend for 28 years to supervise contractors, tile setters, welders, stonecutters, ironworkers, woodcarvers, and other artisans. From 1919 to 1947, Morgan's office produced more than ten thousand architectural drawings for the project. There were also more than a thousand documents written between client and architect, evidence of an incredible working relationship.

In 1957, the Hearst Corporation donated Hearst Castle to the State of California for the enjoyment of the public. It reveals the fascinating lifestyle of one of the most influential and affluent men of his time. Today, this great American country house may be appreciated not only for its magnificent architecture, but also for its grandly designed interiors that integrate Hearst's priceless art and antiques collections.

National Historic Landmark

California Historical Landmark

Listed on the National Register of Historic Places

Owned by the State of California

Operated by the State of California Department of Parks and Recreation as Hearst San Simeon State Historical Monument

Hearst Castle is open year-round and visited by millions each year.

LEFT Casa del Mar *was Hearst's residence beginning in 1923. He moved to* Casa Grande's Gothic Suite *in 1928, but returned to* Casa del Mar *from 1945 to 1947. This cottage featured the most opulent gold-leaf decoration, designed by Julia Morgan and inspired by Italian and Spanish Renaissance motifs.*

OPPOSITE Casa del Monte *was sited to ensure that its large north-facing windows all provided breathtaking views of the California mountains.*

FOLLOWING PAGES
A heady scent of jasmine, roses, and orange blossoms is carried on the breezes through the lush gardens that surround the hilltop paradise of La Cuesta Encantada. *Hearst paid particular attention to the landscaping of his Mediterranean village to optimize a setting worthy of its art and architecture.*

ACKNOWLEDGMENTS

SPECIAL THANKS go to many people who helped this book come to fruition. Photographer David Glomb, with whom it was a blast to work, has produced glorious images that truly reveal the magnificence of these great houses and their gardens. Rizzoli editor Douglas Curran, whose humaneness and people skills I greatly admire, has expertly guided the project from start to finish. Associate publisher David Morton, as always, has been supportive and inspirational. Publisher Charles Miers has given the green light on this project with enthusiasm. And Abigail Sturges, the book's exceptional designer, has once again produced a beautiful piece of artwork.

I would also like to thank the individual owners who have made these spectacular houses their homes and so graciously opened them for this book. The care and generosity of time and the funds with which massive and meticulous restoration and renovation work was accomplished is astounding. It was a pleasure for photographer David Glomb and me to hear your stories and experience your beloved homes.

I am especially grateful to the directors, curators, public relations and communication coordinators, and docents working for the foundations, nonprofits, and the state, which own some of the most important examples of historic domestic architecture in California. Your enthusiasm for each historic house and generosity of spirit in sharing your wealth of knowledge was not only helpful but also inspiring.

My thanks also go to my husband, David, for his concern and support, and to friends and new acquaintances whose hospitality, encouragement, and creative ideas I greatly appreciate.

Especially helpful at critical moments were these knowledgeable realtors: Jeff Hyland, Hilton, Hyland Real Estate, Beverly Hills; Christophe Choo, Christophe Choo Real Estate, Beverly Hills; Jo Ann Mermis and Wes St. Clair, Prudential California Realty, Montecito; Omid Khaki, Sotheby's International Realty, Montecito; and Emily McBride, Village Properties, Montecito.

Laura and Eli Adler, San Anselmo

Anthony Bruce, executive director, Berkeley Architectural Heritage Association

California State Parks: Pati Brown, project manager, Capital District State Museums & Historic Parks, Sacramento

Karin Campion, architectural designer, Sonoma

Richard Cardello, Cardello Design, San Francisco

Christophe Choo, Christophe Choo Real Estate, Beverly Hills

Norman Colavincenzo, Santa Barbara

Kellam de Forest, Santa Barbara

Robert and Leslie Demler, Sonoma

Michael De Rose, architectural designer, Santa Barbara

Filoli House and Gardens, Woodside: Christina Syrett, director, media and public relations; Tom Rogers, former curator

Gamble House, Pasadena: Edward Bosley, Director

Pat Gebhard, author, Santa Barbara

Roc Glomano, Louise, Josephine, Esme and Camille, Rancho Mirage and Delaplane, Virginia

Foster Goldstrom, Berkeley

Frank Goss, Sullivan & Goss Fine Art, Santa Barbara

Hearst Castle, Hearst San Simeon State Historical Monument: Hoyt Fields, museum director; Angela Gutgesell, security; Jim Allen, marketing

Margot Hirsch, San Francisco

Huntington Library, Art Collections and Botanical Gardens, San Marino: Lisa Blackburn, communications coordinator

Jeff Hyland, owner, realtor, Hilton Hyland Real Estate, Beverly Hills

Jerry and Michele Jackman, Santa Barbara

Leland Stanford Mansion State Historic Park, Sacramento: Casey Hayden, director

Lou Henry Hoover House, Stanford University, Stanford: Kathleen M. Baldwin, property manager; Trish Benson, former House Manager; Karen Holiman, new house manager; Laura Jones, director, heritage services & Special projects, University Archaeologist, Land, Buildings, and Real Estate

Omid Khaki, realtor, Sotheby's International Realty, Montecito

Heather King, San Francisco

Mary Liles, Hume, Virginia

Dana and Rain Longo, Santa Barbara

Carter Lowrie, San Francisco

Anne Lynde, Hillsborough

Marin County Civic Center: California Room, Free Library

Joanne McIlwraith, San Francisco

Jo Ann Mermis, realtor, Prudential California Realty, Montecito

Blanca Naranjo, San Marino

David Pashley, Delaplane, Virginia

Paul Price, Carolands historian, Berkeley

Paul Rocheleau, photographer, Richmond, Massachusetts

William Ryan, San Francisco

Bill, Carol, and Fiona Ryder, Arcata

Clarisa and Wes Ru, San Marino

San Mateo County History Museum: Diane Rummel, director; Carol Peterson, archives

Santa Barbara Trust for Historic Preservation: Jarrell C. Jackman, executive director; Michael Imwalle, senior archaeologist; Kendra Rhodes, associate director of development

Andrew Skurman, Andrew Skurman Architects, San Francisco

Wes St. Clair, realtor, Prudential California Realty, Montecito

University of California Santa Barbara, Architectural Drawing Collection, University Art Museum: Melinda Gandara, archivist

USC School of Architecture: Dottie O'Carroll, executive director of advancement

Marcello Villano, Rancho Mirage

Villa di Lemma: Barbara Nimmo, Santa Barbara

Tina Weiss, San Marino

Romy Wyllie, author, Pasadena

Karin Young, San Francisco

RESOURCES

Boutelle, Sara Holmes. *Julia Morgan Architect: Revised and Updated*. New York: Abbeville Press, 1995.

Cardwell, Kenneth H. *Bernard Maybeck: Artisan, Architect, Artist*. Santa Monica: Hennessey + Ingalls, 1996.

Coffman, Taylor. *Hearst Castle: The Story of William Randolph Hearst and San Simeon*. Santa Barbara, California: Sequoia Communications, 1985.

Dwyer, Michael Middleton; Charles Davey, editor. *Carolands: Ernest Sanson, Achille Duchêne, Willis Polk*. San Mateo, California: San Mateo County Historical Association with The Institute of Classical Architecture & Classical America, 2006.

Federal Writers' Project of the Works Progress Administration for the State of California. *The WPA Guide to California*. New York: Pantheon Books, 1984.

Hertrich, William. *The Huntington Botanical Gardens 1905–1949: Personal Recollections of William Hertrich*. San Marino: The Huntington Library, 1949, and Henry E. Huntington Library and Art Gallery, 1988.

Holden, William M. *Sacramento: Excursions into Its History and Natural World*. Fair Oaks, California: Two Rivers Publishing Company, 1988.

Kastner, Victoria. *Hearst Castle: The Biography of a Country House*. New York: Harry N. Abrams, Incorporated, 2000.

Ketcham, Diana. Oakland Fire. Chicago Tribune/New York Times News Service, November 24, 1991.

Knight, Christopher. "Huntington v 2.0" Los Angeles, *The Los Angeles Times*, May 25, 2008, pp. 1, 8–9.

Loe, Nancy E. *Hearst Castle: An Interpretive History of William Randolph Hearst's San Simeon Estate*. Bishop, California: Companion Press, 1994.

Makinson, Randall L. *Greene & Greene: The Blacker House*. Salt Lake City, Utah: Gibbs Smith, Publisher, 2000.

Muchnic, Suzanne. "Taking Up a Broader Mission." Los Angeles: *The Los Angeles Times*, May 25, 2008, p. 7.

Nordhoff, Charles. *California for Health, Pleasure, and Residence: A Book for Travellers and Settlers*. Berkeley, California: Ten Speed Press, 1973 (reprint of original).

Ryan, Catherine and Gary Weimberg, producers and directors. "Three Women and a Château" (DVD). San Mateo: Luna Productions and Inyo Productions in association with the San Mateo County Historical Association, 2006.

Saladino, John F. *Villa*. London: Frances lincoln Publisher, 2009.

Santa Barbara Conservancy. *Images of America: Stone Architecture in Santa Barbara*. Charleston, SC; Chicago; Portsmouth, NH; San Francisco: Arcadian Publishing, 2009.

Spurgeon, Selena A. *Henry Edwards Huntington: His Life and His Collections*. San Marino: Huntington Library, 2008.

Svanevik, Michael and Shirley Burgett. "Charles Templeton Crocker: Thespian at Heart," *The Hillsborough Newsletter*. Town of Hillsborough: Hillsborough, California, 4th Quarter 2008.

Sweeney, Robert. *Casa del Herrero: The Romance of Spanish Colonial*. New York: Rizzoli International Publications, Inc., 2009.

Troutman, Keri Hayes. "Guy Hyde Chick House: Channeling Bernard Maybeck," *Oakland Magazine*. Alameda, California: Alameda Publishing Co., January–February 2007.

Turner, Paul V. *Mrs. Hoover's Pueblo Walls: The Primitive and the Modern in the Lou Henry Hoover House*. Stanford: Stanford University Press, 2004.

Woodbridge, Sally B. *Bernard Maybeck: Visionary Architect*. New York, London, Paris: Abbeville Press Publishers, 1992.

Wyllie, Romy. *Bertram Goodhue: His Life and Residential Architecture*. New York, London: W. W. Norton Company, 2007.

INDEX